A Handful of Stars
Texts That Have
Moved Great Minds

Frank W. Boreham

Contents

BY WAY OF INTRODUCTION 7
I WILLIAM PENN'S TEXT 9
II ROBINSON CRUSOE'S TEXT 17
III JAMES CHALMERS' TEXT 25
IV SYDNEY CARTON'S TEXT 32
V EBENEZER ERSKINE'S TEXT 40
VI DOCTOR DAVIDSON'S TEXT 48
VII HENRY MARTYN'S TEXT 54
VIII MICHAEL TREVANION'S TEXT 62
IX HUDSON TAYLOR'S TEXT 70
X RODNEY STEELE'S TEXT 78
XI THOMAS HUXLEY'S TEXT 86
XII WALTER PETHERICK'S TEXT 94
XIII DOCTOR BLUND'S TEXT 102
XIV HEDLEY VICARS' TEXT 109
XV SILAS WRIGHT'S TEXT 117
XVI MICHAEL FARADAY'S TEXT 124
XVII JANET DEMPSTER'S TEXT 131
XVIII CATHERINE BOOTH'S TEXT 138
XIX UNCLE TOM'S TEXT 145
XX ANDREW BONAR'S TEXT 152
XXI FRANCIS D'ASSISI'S TEXT 159
XXII EVERYBODY'S TEXT 167

A HANDFUL OF STARS
TEXTS THAT HAVE MOVED GREAT MINDS

BY

Frank W. Boreham

A HANDFUL OF STARS
TEXTS THAT HAVE MOVED GREAT MINDS
BY
F. W. BOREHAM

BY WAY OF INTRODUCTION

It is not good that a book should be alone: this is a companion volume to ***A Bunch of Everlastings***. 'O God,' cried Caliban from the abyss,

O God, if you wish for our love,
Fling us ***a handful of stars***!

The Height evidently accepted the challenge of the Depth. Heaven hungered for the love of Earth, and so the stars were thrown. I have gathered up a few, and, like children with their beads and berries, have threaded them upon this string. It will be seen that they do not all belong to the same constellation. Most of them shed their luster over the stern realities of life: a few glittered in the firmament of fiction. It matters little. A great romance is a portrait of humanity, painted by a master-hand. When the novelist employs the majestic words of revelation to transfigure the lives of his characters, he does so because, in actual experience, he finds those selfsame words indelibly engraven upon the souls of men. And, after all, ***Sydney Carton's Text*** is really ***Charles Dickens' Text***; ***Robinson Crusoe's Text*** is ***Daniel Defoe's Text***; the text that stands embedded in the pathos of ***Uncle Tom's Cabin*** is the text that Mrs. Harriet Beecher Stowe had enthroned within her heart. Moreover, to whatever group these splendid orbs belong, their deathless radiance has been derived, in every case, from the perennial Fountain of all Beauty and Brightness.

Frank W. Boreham.
Armadale, Melbourne, Australia.

I
WILLIAM PENN'S TEXT

I

The Algonquin chiefs are gathered in solemn conclave. They make a wild and striking and picturesque group. They are assembled under the widespreading branches of a giant elm, not far from the banks of the Delaware. It is easy to see that something altogether unusual is afoot. Ranging themselves in the form of a crescent, these men of scarred limbs and fierce visage fasten their eyes curiously upon a white man who, standing against the bole of the elm, comes to them as white man never came before. He is a young man of about eight and thirty, wearing about his lithe and well-knit figure a sash of skyblue silk. He is tall, handsome and of commanding presence. His movements are easy, agile and athletic; his manner is courtly, graceful and pleasing; his voice, whilst deep and firm, is soft and agreeable; his face inspires instant confidence. He has large lustrous eyes which seem to corroborate and confirm every word that falls from his lips. These tattooed warriors read him through and through, as they have trained themselves to do, and they feel that they can trust him. In his hand he holds a roll of parchment. For this young man in the skyblue sash is William Penn. He is making his famous treaty with the Indians. It is one of the most remarkable instruments ever completed. 'It is the only treaty,' Voltaire declares, 'that was ever made without an oath, and the only treaty that never was broken.' By means of this treaty with the Indians, William Penn is beginning to realize the greatest aspiration of his life. For William Penn has set his heart on being the Conqueror of the World!

II

Strangely enough, it was a Quaker who fired the young man's fancy with this proud ambition. Thomas Loe was William Penn's good angel. There seemed to be no reason why their paths should cross, yet their paths were always crossing. A subtle and inexplicable magnetism drew them together. Penn's father--Sir William Penn--was an admiral, owning an estate in Ireland. When William was but a small boy, Thomas Loe visited Cork. The coming of the Quaker caused a mild sensation; nobody knew what to make of it. Moved largely by curiosity, the admiral invited the quaint preacher to visit him. He did so, and, before leaving, addressed the assembled household. William was too young to understand, but he was startled when, in the midst of the address, a colored servant wept aloud. The boy turned in his astonishment to his father, only to notice that tears were making their way down the bronzed cheeks of the admiral. The incident filled him with wonder and perplexity. He never forgot it. It left upon his mind an indelible impression of the intense reality of all things spiritual. As a schoolboy, he would wander in the forests that so richly surrounded his Essex home, and give himself to rapt and silent contemplation. On one occasion, he tells us, he 'was suddenly surprised with an inward comfort.' It seemed to him as if a heavenly glory irradiated the room in which he was sitting. He felt that he could never afterwards doubt the existence of God nor question the possibility of the soul's access to Him.

It was at Oxford that the boy's path crossed that of the Quaker for the *second* time. When, as a lad of sixteen, William Penn went up to the University, he found to his surprise that Oxford was the home of Thomas Loe. There the good man had already suffered imprisonment for conscience sake. The personality of the Quaker appealed to the reflective temperament of the young student, whilst the good man's sufferings for his convictions awoke his profoundest sympathies. To the horror of his father, he ardently espoused the persecuted cause, involving himself in such disfavor with the authorities of the University that they peremptorily ordered his dismissal.

But it was the third crossing of the paths that most deeply and permanently affected the destinies of William Penn. Soon after his expulsion from Oxford, he was appointed Victualler of the Squadron lying off Kinsale, and was authorized to reside at, and manage, his father's Irish estate. It was whilst he was thus engaged that Thomas Loe re-visited Cork. Penn, of course, attended the meetings. 'It was in this way,' he tells us, 'that God, in His everlasting kindness, guided my feet in the flower of my youth, when about two and twenty years of age. He visited me with a certain testimony of His eternal Word through a Quaker named Thomas Loe.' The text at that memorable and historic service, like a nail in a sure place, fastened itself upon the mind of the young officer. Thomas Loe preached from the words: '*This is the victory that overcometh the world, even our faith.*'

The faith that overcomes!
The faith by which a man may conquer the world!
The faith that is itself a victory!
'*This is the victory that overcometh the world, even our faith!*'

Penn was electrified. His whole being was stirred to its depths. 'The undying fires of enthusiasm at once blazed up within him,' one record declares. 'He was exceedingly reached and wept much,' the Quaker chronicle assures us. He renounced every hope that he had ever cherished in order that he might realize this one. This was in 1666--the year in which London was devoured by the flames.

'Penn's conversion,' says Dr. Stoughton, 'was now completed. That conversion must not be regarded simply as a change of opinion. It penetrated his moral nature. It made him a new man. He rose into another sphere of spiritual life and consciousness.'

In his lecture on ***Evangelist***, Dr. Alexander Whyte says that the first minister whose words were truly blessed of God for our awakening and conversion has always a place of his own in our hearts. Thomas Loe certainly had a place peculiarly his own in the heart of William Penn. Penn was with him at the last.

'Stand true to God!' cried the dying Quaker, as he clasped the hand of his most notable convert. 'Stand faithful for God! There is no other way! This is the way in which the holy men of old all walked. Walk in it and thou shalt prosper! Live for God and He will be with you! I can say no more. The love of God overcomes my heart!'

The love that overcomes!

The faith that overcomes!
'This is the victory that overcometh the world, even our faith!'

III

William Penn realized his dream. He became the Conqueror of the World. Indeed, he conquered not one world, but two. Or perhaps, after all, they were merely two hemispheres of the selfsame world. One was the World **Within**; the other was the World **Without**; and, of the two, the *first* is always the harder to conquer.

The victory that overcometh **the world**! What is **the world**? The Puritans talked much about **the world**; and Penn was the contemporary of the Puritans. Cromwell died just as the admiral was preparing to send his son to Oxford. Whilst at Cork, Penn sat listening to Thomas Loe's sermon on **the faith that overcometh the world**, John Milton was putting the finishing touches to **Paradise Lost**, and John Bunyan was languishing in Bedford Gaol. Each of the three had something to say about **the world**. To Cromwell it was, as he told his daughter, 'whatever cooleth thine affection after Christ.' Bunyan gave his definition of **the world** in his picture of Vanity Fair. Milton likened **the world** to an obscuring mist--a fog that renders dim and indistinct the great realities and vitalities of life. It is an atmosphere that chills the finest delicacies and sensibilities of the soul. It is too subtle and too elusive to be judged by external appearances. In his fine treatment of **the world**, Bishop Alexander cites, by way of illustration, still another of the contemporaries of William Penn. He paints a pair of companion pictures. He depicts a gay scene at the frivolous and dissolute Court of Charles the Second; and, beside it, he describes a religious assembly of the same period. The *first* gathering appears to be altogether worldly: the *second* has nothing of **the world** about it. Yet, he says, Mary Godolphin lived her life at Court without being tainted by any shadow of worldliness, whilst many a man went up to those solemn assemblies with **the world** raging furiously within his soul!

William Penn saw **the world** in his heart that day as he listened to Thomas Loe; and, in order that he might overcome it, he embraced the faith that the Quaker proclaimed. '***This is the victory that overcometh the world, even our faith.***' And by that faith he overcame ***the world***. Many years afterwards he himself told the story.

'The Lord first appeared to me,' he says, in his ***Journal***, 'in the twelfth year of my age, and He visited me at intervals afterwards and gave me divine impressions of Himself. He sustained me through the darkness and debauchery of Oxford, through all my experiences in France, through the trials that arose from my father's harshness, and through the terrors of the Great Plague. He gave me a deep sense of the vanity of the world and of the irreligiousness of the religions of it. The glory of the world often overtook me, and I was ever ready to give myself up to it.' But, invariably, ***the faith that overcometh the world*** proved victorious. In his monumental ***History of the United States***, Bancroft says that, splendid as were the triumphs of Penn, his greatest conquest was the conquest of his own soul. Extraordinary as was the greatness of his mind; remarkable, both for universality and precision, as were the vast conceptions of his genius; profound as was his scholarship, and astute as was his diplomacy; the historian is convinced that, in the last resort, his greatest contribution to history is the development and influence of his impressive and robust character. 'He was prepared for his work,' Bancroft says, 'by the severe discipline of life; and love without dissimulation formed the basis of his being. The sentiment of cheerful humanity was irrepressibly strong in his bosom; benevolence gushed prodigally from his ever overflowing heart; and when, in his late old age, his intellect was impaired and his reason prostrated, his sweetness of disposition rose serenely over the clouds of disease.' The winsomeness of his ways and the courtliness of his bearing survived for many months the collapse of his memory and the loss of his powers of speech.

Such was his faith's ***first*** victory. It was the conquest of the world ***within***.

IV

'***This is the victory that overcometh the world, even our faith.***' It was by his faith that he obtained his ***second*** great triumph--his conquest of the world ***without***. He disarmed nations by confiding in them. He bound men to himself by trusting them. He vanquished men by believing in them. It was always by his faith that he overcame.

When the admiral died, the nation was in his debt to the extent of sixteen thousand pounds. This amount--on its recovery--Sir William bequeathed to his son. In due time the matter was compounded, William Penn agreeing to accept an immense belt of virgin forest in North America in full settlement of his claim. He resolved to establish a new colony across the seas under happier conditions than any State had ever known. It should be called Pennsylvania; it should be the land of freedom; its capital should be named Philadelphia--the City of Brotherly Love. He was reminded that his first task would be to subdue the Indians. The savages, everybody said, must be conquered; and William Penn made up his mind to conquer them; but he determined to conquer them in his own way. '***This is the victory that overcometh the world, even our faith.***' The Indians were accustomed to slaughter. They understood no language but the language of the tomahawk and the scalping-knife. Ever since the white man had landed on American shores, the forests had resounded with the war-whoops of the tribesmen. One night a colonial settlement had been raided by the red men: the next an Indian village had been burned, and its inhabitants massacred by the outraged whites. The Indians looked with hatred upon the smoke of the English settlements; the settlers dreaded the forests which protected the ambush, and secured the retreat of their murderous foes. William Penn conquered the Indians, and conquered them--according to his text--***by his faith***. 'He will always be mentioned with honor,' Macaulay says, 'as a founder of a colony who did not, in his dealings with a savage people, abuse the strength derived from civilization, and as a lawgiver who, in an age of persecution, made religious liberty the cornerstone of his policy.'

Immediately upon his arrival he called the Indians to meet him. They gathered under the great elm at Shakamaxon--a spot that is now marked by a monument. He approached the chiefs unarmed; and they, in return, threw away their bows and arrows. Presents were exchanged and speeches made. Penn told the natives that he desired nothing but their friendship. He undertook that neither he nor any of his friends should ever do the slightest injury to the person or the property of an Indian; and they, in reply, bound themselves 'to live in love with Onas'--as they called him--'and with the children of Onas, as long as the sun and the moon shall endure.' 'This treaty of peace and friendship was made,' as Bancroft says, 'under the open sky, by the side of the Delaware, with the sun and the river and the forest for witnesses. It was not confirmed by an oath; it was not ratified by signatures and seals; no written record of the conference can be found; and its terms and conditions had no abiding monument, but on the heart. *There* they were written like the law of God and were never forgotten. The simple sons of the wilderness, returning to their wigwams, kept the history of the covenant by strings of wampum, and, long afterwards, in their cabins, they would count over the shells on a clean piece of bark and recall to their own memory, and repeat to their children or to the stranger, the words of William Penn.' The world laughed at the fantastic agreement; but the world noticed, at the same time, that, whilst the neighboring colonies were being drenched in blood and decimated by the barbarity of the Mohicans and the Delawares, the hearths of Pennsylvania enjoyed an undisturbed repose. No drop of Quaker blood was ever shed by an Indian. So complete was the victory of the faith of William Penn!

Nor was the conquest merely negative. When, after a few years, the Quakers began to swarm across the Atlantic to people the new settlement, they were confronted by experiences such as await all pioneers, in young colonies. There were times of stress and privation and hardship. The stern voice of necessity commanded even delicate women to undertake tasks for which their frames were far too frail. In that emergency the Indians came to the rescue. The red men worked for them, trapped for them, hunted for them, and served them in a thousand ways. 'You are all the children of Onas!' they said. Nothing delighted the Indians more than to receive the great Onas as their guest. A feast was arranged in the depths of the forest, bucks were killed, cakes were cooked, and the whole tribe abandoned itself to festivity and rejoicing. And when, years afterwards, they heard that Onas was dead, they sent his widow a characteristic message of sympathy, accompanied by a present of beautiful furs. 'These skins,' they said, 'are to protect you whilst passing through the thorny wilderness without your guide.' The story of the founding of Pennsylvania is, as a classical writer finely says, 'one of the most beautiful incidents in the history of the age.' It was the victory of faith--***the faith that overcometh the world***!

V

'This is the Victory!'
'The Victory that overcometh the World!'
The World Within! The World Without!
'His character always triumphed,' says Bancroft. 'His name was fondly cherished as a household word in the cottages of the old world; and not a tenant of a wigwam from the Susquehannah to the sea doubted his integrity. His fame is as wide as the world: he is one of the few who have gained abiding glory.'
The Conquest of the world!
'Nobody doubted his integrity!'
'He gained abiding glory!'
'This is the Victory that overcometh the World, even our Faith!'

II
ROBINSON CRUSOE'S TEXT

I

During the years that Robinson Crusoe spent upon the island, his most distinguished visitor was a text. Three times it came knocking at the door of his hut, and at the door of his heart. It came to him as his ***doctor*** in the day of sore sickness; it came as his ***minister*** when his soul was in darkness and distress; and it came as his ***deliverer*** in the hour of his most extreme peril.

Nine months after the shipwreck Crusoe was overtaken by a violent fever. His situation filled him with alarm, for he had no one to advise him, no one to help him, no one to care whether he lived or died. The prospect of death filled him with ungovernable terror.

'Suddenly,' he says, 'it occurred to my thought that the Brazilians take no physic but tobacco for all their distempers, and I remembered that I had a roll of tobacco in one of the chests that I had saved from the wreck. I went, directed by heaven no doubt; for in this chest I found a cure both for soul and body. I opened the chest and found the tobacco that I was looking for; and I also found a Bible which, up to this time, I had found neither leisure nor inclination to look into. I took up the Bible and began to read. Having opened the book casually, the first words that occurred to me were these: "***Call upon Me in the day of trouble, and I will deliver thee, and thou shalt glorify Me.***" The words were very apt to my case. They made a great impression upon me and I mused upon them very often. I left my lamp burning in the cave lest I should want anything in the night, and went to bed. But before I lay down I did what I never had done in all my life--I kneeled down and prayed. I asked God to fulfil the promise to me that if I called upon Him in the day of trouble He would deliver me.'

Those who have been similarly situated know what such prayers are worth. 'When the devil was sick the devil a saint would be.' Crusoe's prayer was the child of his terror. He was prepared to snatch at anything which might stand between him and a lonely death. When he called for deliverance, he meant deliverance from sickness and solitude; but it was not of *that* deliverance that the text had come to speak. When, therefore, the crisis had passed, the text repeated its visit. It came to him in time of health.

'Now,' says Crusoe, 'I began to construe the words that I had read--"**Call upon Me in the day of trouble, and I will deliver thee, and thou shalt glorify Me**"--in a different sense from what I had done before. For then I had no notion of any deliverance but my deliverance from the captivity I was in. But now I learned to take it in another sense. Now I looked back upon my past life with such horror, and my sins appeared so dreadful, that my soul sought nothing of God but deliverance from the load of guilt that bore down all my comfort. As for my lonely life, it was nothing. I did not so much as pray for deliverance from my solitude; it was of no consideration in comparison with deliverance from my sin.'

This **second** visit of the text brought him, Crusoe tells us, a great deal of comfort. So did the third. That **third** memorable visit was paid eleven years later. Everybody remembers the stirring story. 'It happened one day, about noon,' Crusoe says. 'I was exceedingly surprised, on going towards my boat, to see the print of a man's naked foot on the shore. I stood like one thunderstruck, or as if I had seen a ghost. I examined it again and again to make sure that it was not my fancy; and then, confused with terror, I fled, like one pursued, to my fortification, scarcely feeling the ground I trod on, looking behind me at every two or three steps, and fancying every stump to be a man.' It was on his arrival at his fortification that the text came to him the third time.

'Lying in my bed,' he says, 'filled with thoughts of my danger from the appearance of savages, my mind was greatly discomposed. Then, suddenly, these words of Scripture came into my thoughts: "**Call upon Me in the day of trouble, and I** *will deliver thee, and thou shalt glorify Me.*" Upon this, rising cheerfully out of my bed, I was guided and encouraged to pray earnestly to God for deliverance. It is impossible to express the comfort this gave me. In answer, I thankfully laid down the Book and was no more sad.'

These, then, were the three visits that the text paid to Crusoe on his desolate island. '***Call upon Me in the day of trouble, and I will deliver thee, and thou shalt glorify Me.***'

When the text came to him the *first* time, he called for deliverance from *sickness*; and was in a few days well.

When the text came to him the *second* time, he called for deliverance from *sin*; and was led to a crucified and exalted Saviour.

When the text came to him the *third* time, he called for deliverance from *savages*; and the savages, so far from hurting a hair of his head, furnished him with his man Friday, the staunchest, truest friend he ever had.

'***Call upon Me****,*' said the text, not once, nor twice, but thrice. And, three times over, Crusoe called, and each time was greatly and wonderfully delivered.

II

Robinson Crusoe was written in 1719; exactly a century later ***The Monastery*** was published. And, significantly enough, the text which shines with such luster in Daniel Defoe's masterpiece forms also the pivot of Sir Walter Scott's weird story. Mary Avenel comes to the climax of her sorrows. She seems to have lost everything and everybody. Her life is desolate; her grief is inconsolable. Her faithful attendant, Tibbie, exhausts herself in futile attempts to compose and comfort the mind of her young mistress. Father Eustace does his best to console her; but she feels that it is all words, words, words. All at once, however, she comes upon her mother's Bible--the Bible that had passed through so many strange experiences and had been so wonderfully preserved. Remembering that this little Book was her mother's constant stay and solace--her counselor in time of perplexity and her comfort in the hour of grief--Mary seized it, Sir Walter says, with as much joy as her melancholy situation permitted her to feel. Ignorant as she was of its contents, she had nevertheless learned from infancy to hold the Volume in sacred veneration. On opening it, she found that, among the leaves, there were texts neatly inscribed in her mother's handwriting. In Mary's present state of mind, these passages, reaching her at a time so critical and in a manner so touching, strangely affected her. She read on one of these slips the consoling exhortation: '***Call upon Me in the day of trouble, and I will deliver thee, and thou shalt glorify Me.***' 'There are those,' Sir Walter says, 'to whom a sense of religion has come in storm and tempest; there are those whom it has summoned amid scenes of revelry and idle vanity; there are those, too, who have heard its still small voice amid rural leisure and placid contentment. But perhaps the knowledge which causeth not to err is most frequently impressed upon the mind during seasons of affliction; and tears are the softened showers which cause the seed of heaven to spring and take root in the human breast. At least, it was thus with Mary Avenel. She read the words--"***Call upon Me in the day of trouble, and I will deliver thee, and thou shalt glorify Me***"--and her heart acquiesced in the conclusion: Surely this is the Word of God!'

In the case of Mary Avenel, the resultant deliverance was as dramatic as in the case of Robinson Crusoe. I turn a few pages of ***The Monastery***, and I come upon this:

'The joyful news that Halbert Glendinning--Mary's lover--still lived was quickly communicated through the sorrowing family. His mother wept and thanked heaven alternately. On Mary Avenel the impression was inconceivably deeper. She had newly learned to pray, and it seemed to her that her prayers had been instantly answered. She felt that the compassion of heaven, which she had learned to implore in the very words of Scripture--"***Call upon Me in the day of trouble, and I will deliver thee, and thou shalt glorify Me***"--had descended upon her after a manner almost miraculous, and recalled the dead from the grave at the sound of her lamentations.'

I lay ***this***, written by Sir Walter Scott, in 1819, beside ***that***, written by Daniel Defoe in 1719. In the mouths of two such witnesses shall every word be established.

III

What was it that led both Daniel Defoe and Sir Walter Scott to give the text such prominence? What was it in the text that appealed so irresistibly to Robinson Crusoe and to Mary Avenel? The answer is fourfold.

1. It was the **Charm of Companionship**. Robinson Crusoe fancied that he was alone upon his island. Mary Avenel fancied that she was left friendless and forsaken. They were both mistaken; and it was the text that showed them their mistake. '*Call upon Me in the day of trouble, and I will deliver thee.*' If such a Deliverer is at hand--so near as to be within sound of their voices--how can Robinson Crusoe be solitary or Mary Avenel forsaken?

 Speak to Him, thou, for He hears; spirit with spirit can meet--   Closer is He than breathing, and nearer than hands and feet!

If there be a shadow of truth in Robinson Crusoe's text, there is no such thing as loneliness for any of us!

2. It was the **Ring of Certainty**. There is a strange and holy dogmatism about the great evangelical promises. '*Call and I will deliver.*' Other physicians say: 'I will come and do my best.' The Great Physician says: 'I will come and heal him.' *The Son of Man is come to seek and to save that which is lost.* He did not embark upon a magnificent effort; He came to do it.

3. It was the **Claim of Monopoly**. 'Call upon *Me* in the day of trouble, and *I* will deliver thee.' It suggests the utter absence of alternatives, of selection, of picking and choosing. In the straits of the soul, the issues are wonderfully simple. There is none other Name given under heaven among men whereby we must be saved. It is *this* Companion--or solitude; *this* Deliverer--or captivity; *this* Saviour--or none.

4. It was the **Absence of Technicality**. '*Call!*'--that is all. '*Call upon Me in the day of trouble, and I will deliver thee, and thou shalt glorify Me!*' *Call!*--as a little child calls for his mother. *Call!*--as a drowning man calls for help. *Call!*--as a frenzied woman calls wildly for succor. There are great emergencies in which we

do not fastidiously choose our words. It is not the mind but the heart that, at such moments, gives to the tongue its noblest eloquence. The prayer that moves Omnipotence to pity, and summons all the hosts of heaven to help, is not the prayer of nicely rounded periods--Faultily faultless, icily regular, splendidly null--but the prayer of passionate entreaty. It is a ***call***--a call such as a doctor receives at dead of night; a call such as the fireman receives when all the alarms are clanging; a call such as the ships receive in mid-ocean, when, hurtling through the darkness and the void, there comes the wireless message, 'S.O.S.' '***Call upon Me in the day of trouble, and I will deliver thee, and thou shalt glorify Me.***' Had the text demanded a tinge of technicality it would have been useless to Robinson Crusoe; it would have mocked the simple soul of poor Mary Avenel. But a call! Robinson Crusoe can call! Mary Avenel can call! Anybody can call! Wherefore, '*call*,' says the text, '***just call, and He will deliver***!'

IV

But I need not have resorted to fiction for a testimony to the value and efficacy of the text--striking and significant as that testimony is. I need have summoned neither Daniel Defoe nor Sir Walter Scott. I could have dispensed with both Robinson Crusoe and Mary Avenel. I could have called a King and Queen to bear all the witness that I wanted.

King Edward the Seventh!

And Queen Alexandra!

For Robinson Crusoe's text is King Edward's text; and Mary Avenel's text is Queen Alexandra's text. There are men and women still living who remember those dark and dreadful days of December, 1871, when it seemed as if the life of King Edward--then Prince of Wales--hung by a single thread. Nobody thought of anything else; the whole world seemed to surround that royal sickbed; the Empire was in a state of breathless suspense. Sunday, the tenth of December, was set aside as a Day of Solemn Intercession, and the strained intensity of the public anxiety reflected itself in crowded but hushed congregations.

And what was going on at the inner heart of things? Early that Sunday morning, the Princess--afterwards Queen Alexandra--opened her Bible and was greeted with these words: '***Call upon Me in the day of trouble, and I will deliver thee, and thou shalt glorify Me.***' A little later, just as the Vicar of Sandringham, the Rev. W. L. Onslow, was preparing to enter his pulpit, he received a note from the Princess. 'My husband being, thank God, somewhat better,' she wrote, 'I am coming to church. I must leave, I fear, before the service is concluded, that I may watch by his bedside. Can you not say a few words in prayer in the early part of the service, that I may join with you in prayer for my husband before I return to him?' The congregation was deeply affected when the Princess appeared, and the rector, with trembling voice, said: 'The prayers of the congregation are earnestly sought for His Royal Highness, the Prince of Wales, who is now most seriously ill.' This was on December the tenth. For the next few days the Prince hovered between life and death. The crisis came on the fourteenth, which, ominously enough, was the anniversary of the death of the Prince Consort. But, whilst the superstitious shook their heads, the Princess clung desperately and believingly to the hope that the text had brought her. And that day, in a way that was almost dramatic, the change came. Sir William Gull, the royal physician, had done all that the highest human skill could suggest; he felt that the issue was now in other hands than his. He was taking a short walk up and down the terrace, when one of the nurses came running to him with pallid face and startled eyes. 'Oh, come, Sir William,' she said, 'there is a change; the Prince is worse!' And, as doctor and nurse hurried together to the sick room, she added bitterly, 'I do not believe God answers prayer! Here is all England praying that he may recover, and he's going to die!' But Sir William Gull's first glance at the Royal patient showed him that the change was for the better. From that moment there was a sure hope of the Prince's recovery, and, by Christmas Day, he was out of danger. Later on, when her husband's restoration was complete, the Princess raised a monument to the deliverance that she had experienced. She presented to the Sandringham Church a brass lectern bearing this inscription: 'To the glory of God; a thank offering for His mercy; 14th December, 1871.--Alexandra. **When I was in trouble I called upon the Lord, and He heard me.**'

Nor is that quite the end of the story. Thirty years later, the Prince ascended the throne. He was to have been crowned on June 26, 1902; but again he was stricken down by serious illness. He recovered, however, and the Coronation took place on the ninth of August. Those familiar with the Coronation Service noticed a striking innovation. The words: '***When I was in trouble, I called upon the Lord, and He heard me***,' were introduced into one of the prayers. 'The words,' Archdeacon Wilberforce afterwards explained, 'were written by the King's own hand, and were used by the Archbishop at His Majesty's express command.'

'***Call upon Me in the day of trouble, and I will deliver thee, and thou shalt glorify Me***,' says the text.

'***When I was in trouble, I called upon the Lord, and He heard me***,' said King Edward and Queen Alexandra.

'I was in trouble through my ***sickness***, and in trouble through my ***sin***,' said Robinson Crusoe, 'and when I called upon the Lord, He heard and delivered me.'

So true is it that ***whosoever shall call on the Name of the Lord, the same shall be saved***.

III
JAMES CHALMERS' TEXT

I

He was 'a broth of a boy,' his biographer tells us. He lived chiefly on boots and boxes. Eager to know what lay beyond the ranges, he wore out more boots than his poor parents found it easy to provide. Taunted by the constant vision of the restless waters, he put out to sea in broken boxes and leaky barrels, that he might follow in the wake of the great navigators. He was a born adventurer. Almost as soon as he first opened his eyes and looked around him, he felt that the world was very wide and vowed that he would find its utmost edges. From his explorations of the hills and glens around his village home, he often returned too exhausted either to eat or sleep. From his ventures upon the ocean he was more than once brought home on a plank, apparently drowned. 'The wind and the sea were his playmates,' we are told; 'he was as much at home in the water as on the land; in fishing, sailing, climbing over the rocks, and wandering among the silent hills, he spent a free, careless, happy boyhood.' Every day had its own romance, its hairbreadth escape, its thrilling adventure.

Therein lies the difference between a man and a beast. At just about the time at which James Chalmers was born in Scotland, Captain Sturt led his famous expedition into the hot and dusty heart of Australia. When he reached Cooper's Creek on the return journey, he found that he had more horses than he would be able to feed; so he turned one of them out on the banks of the creek and left it there. When Burke and Wills reached Cooper's Creek twenty years later, the horse was still grazing peacefully on the side of the stream, and looked up at the explorers with no more surprise or excitement than it would have shown if but twenty hours had passed since it last saw human faces. It had found air to breathe and water to drink and grass to nibble; what did it care about the world? But with man it is otherwise. He wants to know what is on the other side of the hill, what is on the other side of the water, what is on the other side of the world! If he cannot go North, South, East and West himself, he must at least have his newspaper; and the newspaper brings all the ends of the earth every morning to his doorstep and his breakfast-table. This, I say, is the difference between a beast and a man; and James Chalmers--known in New Guinea as the most magnificent specimen of humanity on the islands--was every inch *a man*.

II

But his text! What was James Chalmers' text? When he was eighteen years of age, Scotland found herself in the throes of a great religious revival. In the sweep of this historic movement, a couple of evangelists from the North of Ireland announce that they will conduct a series of evangelistic meetings at Inverary. But Chalmers and a band of daring young spirits under his leadership feel that this is an innovation which they must strenuously resist. They agree to break up the meetings. A friend, however, with much difficulty persuades Chalmers to attend the first meeting and judge for himself whether or not his project is a worthy one.

'It was raining hard,' he says, in some autobiographical notes found among his treasures after the massacre, 'it was raining hard, but I started; and on arriving at the bottom of the stairs I listened whilst they sang "All people that on earth do dwell" to the tune "Old Hundred," and I thought I had never heard such singing before--so solemn, yet so joyful. I ascended the steps and entered. There was a large congregation and all intensely in earnest. The younger of the evangelists was the first to speak. He announced as his text the words: "***The Spirit and the Bride say, Come; and let him that heareth say, Come; and let him that is athirst come; and whosoever will, let him take the water of life freely.***" He spoke directly to me. I felt it much; but at the close I hurried away back to town. I returned the Bible to the friend who, having persuaded me to go, had lent it to me, but I was too upset to speak much to him.'

On the following Sunday night, he was, he says, 'pierced through and through, and felt lost beyond all hope of salvation.' On the Monday, the local minister, the Rev. Gilbert Meikle, who had exercised a deep influence over his early childhood, came to see him and assured him that the blood of Jesus Christ, God's Son, could cleanse him from all sin. This timely visit convinced him that deliverance was at any rate possible. Gradually he came to feel that the voices to which he was listening were, in reality, the Voice of God. 'Then,' he says, 'I believed unto salvation.'

'*He felt that the voices to which he was listening were, in reality, the Voice of God.*' That is precisely what the text says. '*The Spirit and the Bride say, Come.*' The Bride only says '*Come*' because the Spirit says '*Come*'; the Church only says '*Come*' because her Lord says '*Come*'; the evangelists only said '*Come*' because the Voice Divine said '*Come*.' 'He felt that the voices to which he was listening were, in reality, the Voice of God, and he believed unto salvation.'

The Spirit said, Come!
The Bride said, Come!
Let him that is athirst come!
'*I was athirst,*' says Chalmers, '*and I came!*'

And thus a great text began, in a great soul, the manufacture of a great history.

III

Forty years later a thrill of horror electrified the world when the cables flashed from land to land the terrible tidings that James Chalmers, the most picturesque and romantic figure in the religious life of his time, had been killed and eaten by the Fly River cannibals. It is the evening of Easter Sunday. It has for years been the dream of his life to navigate the Fly River and evangelize the villages along its banks. And now he is actually doing it at last. 'He is away up the Fly River,' wrote Robert Louis Stevenson. 'It is a desperate venture, but he is quite a Livingstone card!' Stevenson thought Chalmers all gold. 'He is a rowdy, but he is a hero. You can't weary me of that fellow. He is as big as a house and far bigger than any church. He took me fairly by storm for the most attractive, simple, brave and interesting man in the whole Pacific.' 'I wonder,' Stevenson wrote to Mrs. Chalmers, 'I wonder if even *you* know what it means to a man like *me*--a man fairly critical, a man of the world--to meet one who represents the essential, and who is so free from the formal, from the grimace.' But I digress. As Stevenson says, Mr. Chalmers is away up the Fly River, a desperate venture! But he is boisterously happy about it, and at sunset on this Easter Sunday evening they anchor off a populous settlement just round a bend of the river. The natives, coming off in their canoes, swarm onto the vessel. With some difficulty, Mr. Chalmers persuades them to leave the ship, promising them that he will himself visit them at daybreak. The savages, bent on treachery and slaughter, pull ashore and quickly dispatch runners with messages to all the villages around. When, early next morning, Mr. Chalmers lands, he is surprised at finding a vast assemblage gathered to receive him. He is accompanied by Mr. Tomkins--his young colleague, not long out from England--and by a party of ten native Christians. They are told that a great feast has been prepared in their honor, and they are led to a large native house to partake of it. But, as he enters, Mr. Chalmers is felled from behind with a stone club, stabbed with a cassowary dagger, and instantly beheaded. Mr. Tomkins and the native Christians are similarly massacred. The villages around are soon the scenes of horrible cannibal orgies. 'I cannot believe it!' exclaimed Dr. Parker from the pulpit of the City Temple, on the day on which the tragic news reached England, 'I cannot believe it! I do not want to believe it! Such a mystery of Providence makes it hard for our strained faith to recover itself. Yet Jesus was murdered. Paul was murdered. Many missionaries have been murdered. When I think of *that* side of the case, I cannot but feel that our honored and noble-minded friend has joined a great assembly. James Chalmers was one of the truly great missionaries of the world. He was, in all respects, a noble and kingly character.' And so it was whispered from lip to lip that James Chalmers, the Greatheart of New Guinea, was dead, dead, dead; although John Oxenham denied it.

Greatheart is dead, they say!   Greatheart is dead, they say!   Nor dead, nor sleeping! He lives on! His name   Shall kindle many a heart to equal flame;   The fire he kindled shall burn on and on   Till all the darkness of the lands be gone,   And all the kingdoms of the earth be won,   And one! A soul so fiery sweet can never die   But lives and loves and works through all eternity.

Yes, *lives* and *loves* and *works*! 'There will be much to do in heaven,' he wrote to an old comrade in one of the last letters he ever penned. 'I guess I shall have good mission work to do; great, brave work for Christ! He will have to find it, for I can be nothing else than a missionary!' And so, perchance, James Chalmers is a missionary still!

IV

Now, underlying this brave story of a noble life and a martyr-death is a great principle; and it is the principle that, if we look, we shall find embedded in the very heart of James Chalmers' text. No law of life is more vital. Let us return to that evangelistic meeting held on that drenching night at Inverary, and let us catch once more those matchless cadences that won the heart of Chalmers! '***The Spirit and the Bride say, Come; and let him that heareth say, Come; and let him that is athirst come; and whosoever will, let him take the water of life freely.***'

'***Let him that is athirst come!***' 'I was athirst,' says Chalmers, 'so I came!'

'***Let him that heareth say, Come!***' James Chalmers *heard*; he felt that he must *say*; that is the connecting link between the evangelistic meeting at Inverary and the triumph and tragedy of New Guinea.

'***Let him that heareth, say!***'--that is the principle embedded in the text. The soul's exports must keep pace with the soul's imports. What I have freely received, I must as freely give. The boons that have descended to me from a remote ancestry I must pass on with interest to a remote posterity. The benedictions that my parents breathed on me must be conferred by me upon my children. '***Let him that heareth, say!***' What comes into the City of Mansoul at Ear Gate must go out again at Lip Gate. The auditor of one day must become the orator of the next. It is a very ancient principle. 'He that reads,' says the prophet, 'must run!' 'He that sees must spread!' With those quick eyes of his, James Chalmers saw this at a glance. He recognized that the kingdom of Christ could be established in no other way. He saw that the Gospel could have been offered him on no other terms. What, therefore, he had with such wonder heard, he began, with great delight, to proclaim. Almost at once he accepted a Sunday school class; the following year he began preaching in those very villages through which, as a boy, his exploratory wanderings had so often taken him; a year later he became a city missionary, that he might pass on the message of the Spirit and the Bride to the teeming poor of Glasgow; and, twelve months later still, he entered college, in order to equip himself for service in the uttermost ends of the earth. His boyish passion for books and boxes had been sanctified at last by his consecration to a great heroic mission.

V

'***Let him that is athirst come!***' 'I was athirst,' says Chalmers, 'and I came!'

'***Let him that heareth say, Come!***' And Chalmers, having heard, said 'Come!' and said it with effect. Dr. Lawes speaks of one hundred and thirty mission stations which he established at New Guinea. And look at this! 'On the first Sabbath in every month not less than three thousand men and women gather devotedly round the table of the Lord, reverently commemorating the event which means so much to them and to all the world. Many of them were known to Chalmers as savages in feathers and war-paint. Now, clothed and in their right mind, the wild, savage look all gone, they form part of the Body of our Lord Jesus Christ and are members of His Church. Many of the pastors who preside at the Lord's Table bear on their breasts the tattoo marks that indicate that their spears had been imbrued with human blood. Now sixty-four of them, thanks to Mr. Chalmers' influence, are teachers, preachers and missionaries.' They, too, having listened, proclaim; having received, give; having heard, say; having been auditors, have now become orators. They have read and therefore they run. Having believed with the heart, they therefore confess with the mouth. This is not only a law of life; it is the law of the life everlasting. It is only by loyalty to this golden rule, on the part of all who hear the Spirit and the Bride say Come, that the kingdoms of this world can become the kingdoms of our God and of His Christ. It is the secret of world-conquest; and, besides it, there is no other.

VI

'The Spirit and the Bride say, Come; and let him that heareth say, Come; and let him that is athirst come; and whosoever will, let him take the water of life freely.'
'Let him that is athirst come!'
'Let him that heareth say, Come!'

I have somewhere read that, out in the solitudes of the great dusty desert, when a caravan is in peril of perishing for want of water, they give one camel its head and let him go. The fine instincts of the animal will lead him unerringly to the refreshing spring. As soon as he is but a speck on the horizon, one of the Arabs mounts his camel and sets off in the direction that the liberated animal has taken. When, in his turn, he is scarcely distinguishable, another Arab mounts and follows. When the loose camel discovers water, the first Arab turns and waves to the second; the second to the third, and so on, until all the members of the party are gathered at the satisfying spring. As each man sees the beckoning hand, he turns and beckons to the man behind him. He that sees, signals; he that hears, utters. It is the law of the life everlasting; it is the fundamental principle of James Chalmers' text and of James Chalmers' life.

'Let him that is athirst come!' 'I was athirst,' says Chalmers, 'so I came!'

I heard the voice of Jesus say, 'Behold, I freely give The living water; thirsty one, Stoop down, and drink, and live.' I came to Jesus, and I drank Of that life-giving stream; My thirst was quenched, my soul revived, And now I live in Him.

'And now I live in Him.' The life that James Chalmers lived in his Lord was a life so winsome that he charmed all hearts, a life so contagious that savages became saints beneath his magnetic influence. He had heard, at Inverary, the Spirit and the Bride say, **Come!** And he esteemed it a privilege beyond all price to be permitted to make the abodes of barbarism and the habitations of cruelty re-echo the matchless music of that mighty monosyllable.

IV
SYDNEY CARTON'S TEXT

I

Memory is the soul's best minister. Sydney Carton found it so. On the greatest night of his life--the night on which he resolved to lay down his life for his friend--a text swept suddenly into his mind, and, from that moment, it seemed to be written everywhere. He was in Paris; the French Revolution was at its height; sixty-three shuddering victims had been borne that very day to the guillotine; each day's toll was heavier than that of the day before; no man's life was safe. Among the prisoners awaiting death in the Conciergerie was Charles Darnay, the husband of her whom Sydney himself had loved with so much devotion but so little hope.

'O Miss Manette,' he had said, on the only occasion on which he had revealed his passion, 'when, in the days to come, you see your own bright beauty springing up anew at your feet, think now and then that there is a man who would give his life to keep a life you love beside you!'

And now that hour had come. It happened that Charles Darnay and Sydney Carton were, in form and feature, extraordinarily alike. Darnay was doomed to die on the guillotine: Carton was free. For the first time in his wayward life, Sydney saw his course clearly before him. His years had been spent aimlessly, but now he set his face like a flint towards a definite goal. He stepped out into the moonlight, not recklessly or negligently, but 'with the settled manner of a tired man who had wandered and struggled and got lost, but who at length struck into his road and saw its end.' He would find some way of taking Darnay's place in the gloomy prison; he would, by his substitution, restore her husband to Lucy's side; he would make his life sublime at its close. His career should resemble a day that, fitful and overcast, ends at length in a glorious sunset. He would save his life by losing it!

It was at that great moment that memory exercised its sacred ministry upon the soul of Sydney Carton. As he paced the silent streets, dark with heavy shadows, the moon and the clouds sailing high above him, he suddenly recalled the solemn and beautiful words which he had heard read at his father's grave: '*I am the Resurrection and the Life; he that believeth in Me, though he were dead, yet shall he live; and whosoever liveth and believeth in Me shall never die.*' Sydney did not ask himself why the words had rushed upon him at that hour, although, as Dickens says, the reason was not far to seek. But he kept repeating them. And, when he stopped, the air seemed full of them. The great words were written across the houses on either side of him; he looked up, and they were inscribed across the dark clouds and the clear sky; the very echoes of his footsteps reiterated them. When the sun rose, it seemed to strike those words--the burden of the night--straight and warm to his heart in its long bright rays. Night and day were both saying the same thing. He heard it everywhere: he saw it in everything--

'*I am the Resurrection and the Life; he that believeth in Me, though he were dead, yet shall he live; and whosoever liveth and believeth in Me shall never die.*'

That was Sydney Carton's text.

II

It is a great thing--a very great thing--to be able to save those you love by dying for them. I well remember sitting in my study at Hobart one evening, when there came a ring at the bell. A moment later a man whom I knew intimately was shown in. I had seen him a few weeks earlier, yet, as I looked upon him that night, I could scarcely believe it was the same man. He seemed twenty years older; his hair was gray; his face furrowed and his back bent. I was staggered at the change. He sat down and burst into tears.

'Oh, my boy, my boy!' he sobbed.

I let him take his time, and, when he had regained his self-possession, he told me of his son's great sin and shame.

'I have mentioned this to nobody,' he said, 'but I could keep it to myself no longer. I knew that you would understand.'

And then he broke down again. I can see him now as he sits there, rocking himself in his agony, and moaning:

'If only I could have died for him! If only I could have died for him!'

But he couldn't! That was the torture of it! I remember how his heart-broken cry rang in my ears for days; and on the following Sunday there was only one subject on which I could preach. ***'And the king was much moved, and went up to the chamber over the gate and wept; and as he went he cried: O my son Absalom! my son, my son Absalom! Would God I had died for thee, O Absalom, my son, my son!'***

It was the unutterable grief of David, and of my poor friend, that they could not save those they loved by dying for them. It was the joy of Sydney Carton that he could! He contrived to enter the Conciergerie; made his way to Darnay's cell; changed clothes with him; hurried him forth; and then resigned himself to his fate. Later on, a fellow prisoner, a little seamstress, approached him. She had known Darnay and had learned to trust him. She asked if she might ride with him to the scaffold.

'I am not afraid,' she said, 'but I am little and weak, and, if you will let me ride with you and hold your hand, it will give me courage!'

As the patient eyes were lifted to his face, he saw a sudden doubt in them, and then astonishment. She had discovered that he was not Darnay.

'Are you dying for him?' she whispered.

'For him--and his wife and child. Hush! Yes!'

'Oh, you will let me hold your brave hand, stranger?'

'Hush! Yes, my poor sister; to the last!'

Nobody has ever read ***A Tale of Two Cities*** without feeling that this was the moment of Sydney Carton's supreme triumph.

'It is,' he said--and they are the last words in the book--'it is a far, far better thing that I do than I have ever done!'

He had never tasted a joy to be compared with this. He was able to save those he loved by dying for them!

That is precisely the joy of the Cross! ***That*** was the light that shone upon the Saviour's path through all the darkness of the world's first Easter. ***That*** is why, when He took the bread and wine--the emblems of His body about to be broken and His blood about to be shed--He gave thanks. It is ***that***--and that alone--that accounts for the fact that He entered the Garden of Gethsemane with a song upon His lips. It was for the joy that was set before Him that He endured the Cross, despising its shame!

'Death!' He said. 'What of Death? *I am the Life*, not only of Myself, but of all who place their hands in Mine!

'The Grave! What of the Grave? *I am the Resurrection!*

'*I am the Resurrection and the Life; he that believeth in Me, though he were dead, yet shall he live; and whosoever liveth and believeth in Me shall never die.*'

He felt that it was a great thing--a very great thing--to be able to save those He loved by dying for them.

III

'*I am the Resurrection!*'--those were the words that Sydney Carton saw written on land and on water, on earth and on sky, on the night on which he made up his mind to die. '*I am the Resurrection!*' They were the words that he had heard read beside his father's grave. They are the words that we echo, in challenge and defiance, over ***all*** our graves. The rubric of the Church of England requires its ministers to greet the dead at the entrance to the churchyard with the words: '*I am the Resurrection and the Life*;' and, following the same sure instinct, the ministers of all the other Churches have adopted a very similar practice. The earth seems to be a garden of graves. We speak of those who have passed from us as 'the great majority.' We appear to be conquered. But it is all an illusion.

'O Grave!' we ask, in every burial service, 'where is thy victory?' And the question answers itself. The victory does not exist. The struggle is not yet ended. '*I am the Resurrection!'*

'*I am the Life!'*--that is what all the echoes were saying as Sydney Carton, cherishing a great heroic purpose in his heart, paced the deserted streets that night.

'*I am the Life! I am the Life!'*
'*He that believeth in Me, though he were dead, yet shall he live!'*
'*Whosoever believeth in Me shall never die!'*

That being so, what does death matter? 'O, death!' we cry, 'where is thy sting?' and once more the question answers itself.

'*O Death, where is thy sting?'--'I am the Life!'*
'*O Grave, where is thy victory?'--'I am the Resurrection!'*
The Life and the Resurrection! '*I am the Resurrection and the Life!'*

The text that he saw in every sight, and heard in every sound, made all the difference to Sydney Carton. The end soon came, and this is how Dickens tells the story.

The tumbrils arrive at the guillotine. The little seamstress is ordered to go first. 'They solemnly bless each other. The thin hand does not tremble as he releases it. Nothing worse than a sweet, bright constancy is in the patient face. She is gone. The knitting women, who count the fallen heads, murmur twenty-two. And then--

'*I am the Resurrection and the Life; he that believeth in Me, though he were dead, yet shall he live; and whosoever liveth and believeth in Me shall never die.'*

They said of him about the city that night that it was the peacefullest man's face ever beheld there. Many added that he looked sublime and prophetic.

I am the Resurrection! O Grave, where is thy victory?
I am the Life! O Death, where is thy sting?

IV

But there was more in Sydney Carton's experience than we have yet seen. It happens that this great saying about **the Resurrection and the Life** is not only Sydney Carton's text; it is Frank Bullen's text; and Frank Bullen's experience may help us to a deeper perception of Sydney Carton's. In his ***With Christ at Sea***, Frank Bullen has a chapter entitled 'The Dawn.' It is the chapter in which he describes his conversion. He tells how, at a meeting held in a sail-loft at Port Chalmers, in New Zealand, he was profoundly impressed. After the service, a Christian worker--whom I myself knew well--engaged him in conversation. He opened a New Testament and read these words: '***I am the Resurrection and the Life; he that believeth in Me, though he were dead, yet shall he live; and whosoever liveth and believeth in Me shall never die.***' The earnest little gentleman pointed out the insistence on faith: the phrase '***believeth in Me***' occurs twice in the text: faith and life go together. Would Frank Bullen exercise that faith?

'Every word spoken by the little man went right to my heart,' Mr. Bullen assures us, 'and, when he ceased, there was an appeal in his eyes that was even more eloquent than his words. But beyond the words and the look was the interpretation of them to me by some mysterious agency beyond my comprehension. For, in a moment, the hidden mystery was made clear to me, and I said quietly, "I see, sir; and I believe!" "Let us thank God!" answered the little man, and together we knelt down by the bench. There was no extravagant joy, no glorious bursting into light and liberty, such as I have read about as happening on those occasions; it was the satisfaction of having found one's way after long groping in darkness and misery--***the way that led to peace***.'

Now the question is: did those words--the words that came with such power to Frank Bullen in the New Zealand sail-loft, and to Sydney Carton in the Paris streets--have the same effect upon both? Did they lead both of them to penitence and faith and peace? I think they did. Let us return to Sydney Carton as the sun is rising on that memorable morning on which he sees the text everywhere. He leaves the streets in which he has wandered by moonlight and walks beside a stream.

'A trading-boat, with a sail of the softened color of a dead leaf, glided into his view, floated by him, and died away. As its silent track in the water disappeared, the prayer that had broken up out of his heart for a merciful consideration of all his poor blindnesses and errors ended in the words: "***I am the Resurrection and the Life.***"'

'***He that believeth in Me ... whosoever believeth in Me!***'--the insistent demand for faith.

'*He that believeth in Me!*'--Sydney Carton believed and found peace.

'*He that believeth in Me!*'--Frank Bullen believed and found peace.

Paul has a classical passage in which he shows that those who have passed through experiences such as these, have themselves '*risen with Christ into newness of life.*'

Risen with Christ! They have found *the Resurrection*!

Newness of life! They have found *the Life*!

In his ***Death in the Desert***, Browning describes the attempts that were made to revive the sinking man. It seemed quite hopeless. The most that he would do was--

To smile a little, as a sleeper does, If any dear one call him, touch his face--
And smiles and loves, but will not be disturbed.

Then, all at once, the boy who had been assisting in these proceedings, moved by some swift inspiration, sprang from his knees and proclaimed a text: '***I am the Resurrection and the Life!***' As if by magic, consciousness revisited the prostrate form; the man opened his eyes; sat up; stared about him; and then began to speak. A wondrous virtue seemed to lurk in the majestic words that the boy recited. By that virtue Sydney Carton, Frank Bullen, and a host of others passed from death into life everlasting.

V

I began by saying that it is a great thing--a very great thing--to be able to save those you love by dying for them.

I close by stating the companion truth. It is a great thing--a very great thing--to have been died for.

On the last page of his book Dickens tells us what Sydney Carton would have seen and said if, on the scaffold, it had been given him to read the future.

'I see,' he would have exclaimed, 'I see the lives for which I lay down my life--peaceful, useful, prosperous and happy--in that England which I shall see no more. I see her with a child upon her bosom who bears my name. I see that I hold ***a sanc-***

tuary in all their hearts, and in the hearts of their descendants, generations hence. I see her, an old woman, weeping for me on the anniversary of this day. I see her and her husband, their course done, lying side by side in their last earthly bed; and I know that each was not more honored and held sacred in the other's soul than I was in the souls of both!'

'I see that I hold *a sanctuary in all their hearts*!'--it is a lovely phrase.

It is a great thing--a very great thing--to have been died for!

Wherefore let each man be at some pains to build in his heart a sanctuary to Him who, for us men and for our salvation, laid down His life with a song!

V
EBENEZER ERSKINE'S TEXT

I

It is a lovely Sunday afternoon in the early summer of the year 1690. The graceful and heathery path that winds its way along the banks of the Tweed, from the stately ruins of Melrose to the crumbling gables of Dryburgh, is in its glory. The wooded track by the waterside is luxuriating in bright sunshine, glowing colors and soft shadows. We are traversing one of the most charming and romantic districts that even Scotland can present. Here 'every field has its battle, every rivulet its song.' More than a century hence, this historic neighborhood is destined to furnish the home, and fire the fancy, of Sir Walter Scott; and here, beneath the vaulted aisle of Dryburgh's ancient abbey, he will find his last resting-place. But that time is not yet. Even now, however, in 1690, the hoary cloister is only a battered and weatherbeaten fragment. It is almost covered by the branches of the trees that, planted right against the walls, have spread their limbs like creepers over the mossy ruins, as though endeavoring to protect the venerable pile. And here, sitting on a huge slab that has fallen from the broken arch above, is a small boy of ten. His name is Ebenezer Erskine; he is the son of the minister of Chirnside. Like his father, he was born here at Dryburgh; and to-day the two are revisiting the neighborhood round which so many memories cluster. This morning the father, the Rev. Henry Erskine, has been catechizing a group of children at the kirk. He selected the questions in the Shorter Catechism that relate to the Ten Commandments; and the very first of the answers that his father then taught him has made a profound impression on Ebenezer's mind. The forty-third question runs: '**What is the preface to the Ten**

Commandments?' And the answer is: '***The preface to the Ten Commandments is in these words: "I am the Lord thy God which have brought thee out of the Land of Egypt, out of the house of bondage."***' Other questions follow, and they, with their attendant answers, have been duly memorized. But they have failed to hold his thought. This one, however, refuses to be shaken off. He has, quite involuntarily, repeated it to himself a hundred times as he pushed his way through the heather to the mossy abbey. It sounds in his ears like a claim, a challenge, an insistent and imperative demand.

I am the Lord!
I am thy God!
The Lord! Thy God!
It is his first realization of the fact that he is not altogether his own.

II

Eighteen years have passed. He is now the minister of the Portmoak parish. But it is a poor business. 'I began my ministry,' he says, 'without much zeal, callously and mechanically, being swallowed up in unbelief and in rebellion against God.' He feels no enthusiasm for the Bible; indeed, the New Testament positively wearies him. His sermons are long and formal; he learns them by heart and repeats them parrot-fashion, taking care to look, not into the faces of his people, but at a certain nail in the opposite wall. Happily for himself and for the world, he has by this time married a wife to whom the truth is no stranger. For years, poor Mrs. Erskine has wept in secret over her husband's unregenerate heart and unspiritual ministry. But now a terrible sickness lays her low. Her brain is fevered; she raves in her delirium; her words are wild and passionate. Yet they are words that smite her husband's conscience and pierce his very soul. 'At last,' so runs the diary, 'the Lord was pleased to calm her spirit and give her a sweet serenity of mind. This, I think, was the first time that ever I felt the Lord touching my heart in a sensible manner. Her distress and her deliverance were blessed to me. Some few weeks after, she and I were sitting together in my study, and while we were conversing about the things of God, the Lord was pleased to rend the veil and to give me a glimmering view of salvation which made my soul acquiesce in Christ as the new and living way to glory.' The old text comes back to him.

'I am the Lord thy God!'
'I am the Lord thy God!'

Once more it sounds like a claim. And this time he yields. He makes his vow in writing. *'I offer myself up, soul and body, unto God the Father, Son and Holy Ghost. I flee for shelter to the blood of Jesus. I will live to Him; I will die to Him. I take heaven and earth to witness that all I am and all I have are His.'*

Thus, on August 26, 1708, Ebenezer Erskine makes his covenant. 'That night,' he used to say, 'I got my head out of Time into Eternity!'

III

Ten more years have passed. It is now 1718; Ebenezer Erskine is thirty-eight. Filled with concern for the souls of his people at Portmoak, he preaches a sermon on the text that had played so great a part in bringing his own spirit out of bondage.

'I am the Lord thy God!'
'I am the Lord thy God!'

As he preaches, the memory of his own experience rushes back upon him. His soul catches fire. He is one moment persuasive and the next peremptory. No sermon that he ever preached made a greater impression on his congregation; and, when it was printed, it proved to be the most effective and fruitful of all his publications.

IV

Five and thirty further years have run their course. Mr. Erskine is now seventy-three. He has passed through the fires of persecution, and, in days of tumult and unrest, has proved himself a leader whom the people have delighted, at any cost, to follow. But his physical frame is exhausted. An illness overtakes him which, continuing for over a year, at last proves fatal. His elders drop in from time to time to read and pray with him. To-day one of them, the senior member of the little band, is moved, in taking farewell of his dying minister, to ask a question of him. After grasping the sick man's hand and moving towards the door, a sudden impulse seizes him and he returns to the bedside.

'You have often given us good advice, Mr. Erskine,' he says, 'as to what we should do with our souls in life and in death; may I ask what you are now doing with your own?'

'I am just doing with it,' the old man replies, 'what I did forty years ago; I am resting it on that word, "*I am the Lord thy God!*"'

V

Now what was it, I wonder, that Ebenezer Erskine saw in this string of monosyllables as he sat on the fallen slab beside the ruined abbey in 1690, as he sat conversing with his convalescent wife in 1708, as he preached with such passion in 1718, and as he lay dying in 1753? What, to him, was the significance of that great sentence that, as the catechism says, forms '***the preface to the Ten Commandments***'? Ebenezer Erskine saw, underlying the words, two tremendous principles. They convinced him that *the Center must always be greater than the Circumference* and they convinced him that *the Positive must always be greater than the Negative*.

The Center must always be greater than the Circumference, for, without the center, there can be no circumference. And there, in the very first word of this 'preface to the Ten Commandments,' stands the august center around which all the mandates revolve. '*I am the Lord thy God.*' 'I have many times essayed,' Luther tells us in his ***Table-Talk***, 'thoroughly to investigate the Ten Commandments; but at the very outset--"*I am the Lord thy God*"--I stuck fast. That single word "*I*" put me to a non-plus.' I am not surprised. The man who would enter this Palace of Ten Chambers will find God awaiting him on the threshold; and he must make up his mind as to his relationship with Him before he can pass on to investigate the interior of the edifice. In learning his Shorter Catechism that Sunday morning at

Dryburgh, Ebenezer Erskine, then a boy of ten, had come face to face with God; and he felt that he dared not proceed to the **Circumference** until his heart was in harmony with the **Center**.

VI

He felt, too, that the **Positive** must precede the **Negative**. The *person* of the most High must come before the *precepts* of the Most High; the **Thou Shalts** must come before the **Thou Shalt Nots**. The superstructure of a personal religion cannot be reared on a foundation of negatives. Life can only be constructed positively. The soul cannot flourish on a principle of subtraction; it can only prosper on a principle of addition. It is at this point that we perpetrate one of our commonest blunders. Between Christmas Day and New Year's Day, we invariably frame a variety of good resolutions; we register a number of excellent resolves. But, for the most part, they come to nothing; and they come to nothing because they are so largely negative. 'I will never again do such-and-such a thing'; 'I will never again behave in such-and-such a way'; and so on. We have failed to discover the truth that gripped the soul of Ebenezer Erskine that day at Dryburgh. He saw, as he repeated to himself his catechism, that the Ten Commandments consist of three parts.

(1) *The Preface--'I am the Lord thy God!'*
(2) *The Precepts--'Thou shalt ...'*
(3) *The Prohibitions--'Thou shall not ...'*

Our New Year's resolutions assume that we should put third things first. We are wrong. As Ebenezer Erskine saw, we must put the **Person** before the **Precepts**, and the **Precepts** before the **Prohibitions**. The **Center** must come before the **Circumference**; the **Positive** before the **Negative**.

When, at the end of December, we pledge ourselves so desperately to do certain things no more, we entirely forget that our worst offenses do not consist in outraging the **Thou Shalt Nots**; our worst offenses consist in violating the **Thou**

Shalts. The revolt of the soul against the divine ***Prohibitions*** is as nothing compared with the revolt of the soul against the divine ***Precepts***; just as the revolt of the soul against the divine ***Precepts*** is as nothing compared with the revolt of the soul against the ***Divine Person***. It is by a flash of real spiritual insight that, in the General Confession in the Church of England Prayer Book, the clause, '***We have left undone those things which we ought to have done***,' precedes the clause, '***And we have done those things which we ought not to have done.***' In his ***Ecce Homo***, Sir John Seeley has pointed out the radical difference between the villains of the parables and the villains that figure in all other literature. In the typical novel the villain is a man who does what he ought not to do; in the tales that Jesus told the villain is a man who leaves undone what he ought to have done. 'The sinner whom Christ denounces,' says Sir John, 'is he who has done nothing; the priest and the Levite who passed by on the other side; the rich man who allowed the beggar to lie unhelped at his gate; the servant who hid in a napkin the talent intrusted to him; the unprofitable hireling who did only what it was his duty to do.' Christ's villains are the men who sin against the ***Person*** and the ***Precepts*** of the Most High; he scarcely notices the men who violate the ***Prohibitions***. Yet it is of the ***Prohibitions*** that, when New Years come, we think so much.

>   At vesper-tide,
> One virtuous and pure in heart did pray,
> 'Since none I wronged in deed or word to-day,
> From whom should I crave pardon? Master, say.'

   A voice replied: 'From the sad child whose joy thou hast not planned; The goaded beast whose friend thou didst not stand; The rose that died for water from thy hand.'
   During a ministry of nearly thirty years, it has been my privilege and duty to deal with men and women of all kinds and conditions. I have attended hundreds of deathbeds. In reviewing those experiences to-day, I cannot remember a single case of a man who found it difficult to believe that God could forgive those things that he ought not to have done and had done; and I cannot recall a single case of a man who found it easy to believe that God could forgive those things that he ought to

have done but had left undone. It is our sins against the divine **Precepts** that sting most venomously at the last:

'The sad, sad child whose joy thou hast not planned; The goaded beast whose friend thou didst not stand; The rose that died for water from thy hand!'

Ebenezer Erskine saw that day at Dryburgh that he must recognize the inspired order. He must bow first of all to the authority of the Divine **Person**; he must recognize the obligations involved in the Divine **Precepts**; and, after this, he must eschew those things that are forbidden by the Divine **Prohibitions**. That order he never forgot.

VII

George Macdonald tells us how, when the Marquis of Lossie was dying, he sent post-haste for Mr. Graham, the devout schoolmaster. Mr. Graham knew his man and went cautiously to work.

'Are you satisfied with yourself my lord?'

'No, by God!'

'You would like to be better?'

'Yes; but how is a poor devil to get out of this infernal scrape?'

'Keep the commandments!'

'That's it, of course; but there's no time!'

'If there were but time to draw another breath, there would be time to begin!'

'How am I to begin? Which am I to begin with?'

'There is one commandment which includes all the rest!'

'Which is that?'

'Believe on the Lord Jesus Christ, and thou shalt be saved!'

What did the schoolmaster mean? He meant that the **Person** must precede the **Precepts**, as the **Precepts** must precede the **Prohibitions**; he was insisting on the divine order; that was all. And I feel confident that *that* was the burden of that powerful sermon that Ebenezer Erskine preached to his people at Portmoak in 1718. His last illness, as I have said, continued for twelve months. It was in its earlier stages that the old elder asked his question and received his minister's testimony concerning the text. A year later Mr. Erskine referred to the words again. On the morning of the first of June, he awoke from a brief sleep, and, seeing his daughter, Mrs. Fisher, sitting reading by his bedside, he asked her the name of the book.

'I am reading one of your own sermons, father!'

'Which one?'

'The one on "*I am the Lord thy God!*"'

'Ah, lass,' he exclaimed, his face lighting up, as a wave of sacred memories swept over him, 'that is the best sermon ever I preached!'

A few minutes later he closed his eyes, slipped his hand under his cheek, composed himself on his pillow, and ceased to breathe. The noble spirit of Ebenezer Erskine was with God.

Ebenezer Erskine reminds me of his great predecessor, Samuel Rutherford. When Rutherford was staying for a while at the house of James Guthrie, the maid was surprised at hearing a voice in his room. She had supposed he was alone. Moved by curiosity, she crept to his door. She then discovered that Rutherford was in prayer. He walked up and down the room, exclaiming, '*O Lord, make me to believe in Thee!*' Then, after a pause, he moved to and fro again, crying, '*O Lord, make me to love Thee!*' And, after a second rest, he rose again, praying, '*O Lord, make me to keep all Thy commandments!*' Rutherford, like Erskine a generation later, had grasped the spiritual significance of the divine order.

'*Make me to believe in Thee!*'--the commandment that, as the schoolmaster told the Marquis, includes all the commandments!

'*Make me to love Thee!*'--for love, as Jesus told the rich young ruler, is the fulfilment of the whole law.

'*Make me to obey all Thy commandments!*'

The man who learns the Ten Commandments at the school of Samuel Rutherford or at the school of Ebenezer Erskine will see a shining path that runs from Mount Sinai right up to the Cross and on through the gates of pearl into the City of God.

VI
DOCTOR DAVIDSON'S TEXT

I

There are only two things worth mentioning in connection with Dr. Davidson, but they are both of them very beautiful. The one was his life: the other was his death. Ian Maclaren tells us that the old doctor had spent practically all his days as minister at Drumtochty. He was the father of all the folk in the glen. He was consulted about everything. Three generations of young people had, in turn, confided to his sympathetic ear the story of their loves and hopes and fears; rich and poor had alike found in him a guide in the day of perplexity and a comforter in the hour of sorrow. And now it is Christmas Day--the doctor's last Christmas--and a Sunday. The doctor had preached as usual in the kirk; had trudged through the snow to greet with seasonable wishes and gifts one or two people who might be feeling lonely or desolate; and now, the day's work done, was entertaining Drumsheugh at the manse. All at once, he began to speak of his ministry, lamenting that he had not done better for his people, and declaring that, if he were spared, he intended to preach more frequently about the Lord Jesus Christ.

'You and I, Drumsheugh, will have to go a long journey soon, and give an account of our lives in Drumtochty. Perhaps we have done our best as men can, and I think we have tried; but there are many things we might have done otherwise, and some we ought not to have done at all. It seems to me now, the less we say in that day of the past, the better. We shall wish for mercy rather than justice, and'--here the doctor looked earnestly over his glasses at his elder--'we would be none the worse, Drumsheugh, of a Friend to say a good word for us both in the Great

Court!'

'A've thocht that masel'--it was an agony for Drumsheugh to speak--'a've thocht that masel mair than aince. Weelum MacLure was ettlin' aifter the same thing the nicht he slippit awa, and gin ony man cud hae stude on his ain feet yonder, it was Weelum.'

It was the doctor's last conversation. When his old servant entered the room next morning, he found his master sitting silent and cold in his chair.

'We need a Friend in the Great Court!' said the doctor.

'A've thocht that masel!' replied Drumsheugh.

'Weelum MacLure was ettlin' after the same thing the nicht he slippit awa!'

'*For there is one God, and one Mediator between God and men, the Man Christ Jesus.*'

II

My Bible contains two stories--one near its beginning and one near its end--which to-day I must lay side by side. The *first* is the story of a man who feels that he is suffering more than his share of the slings and arrows of outrageous fortune. He thinks of God as very high and very holy; too wise to err and too good to be unkind; yet he cannot shake from his mind the conviction that God has misunderstood him. And, in his agony, he cries out for one who can arbitrate between his tortured soul and the God who seems to be so angry with him. Oh, for one a little less divine than God, yet a little less human than himself, who could act as an adjudicator, an umpire, a mediator between them! But neither the heavens above nor the earth beneath can produce one capable of ending the painful controversy. 'There is no daysman who can come between us and lay his hand upon us both!'

A God!
But no Mediator!
That is the *first* story.

The *second* story, the story from the end of the Bible, is the story of an old minister whose life-work is finished. He writes, in a reminiscent vein, to a young minister who is just beginning; and earnestly refers to his own ordination. 'Whereunto,' he asks, 'was I ordained a preacher and an apostle and a teacher of the Gentiles in faith and verity?' What is his message? He answers his own question. It is this. '***For there is one God, and one Mediator between God and men, the Man Christ Jesus.***'

A God!

And a Mediator!

Job needed a Friend in the Great Court; but, alas, he could not find one!

Paul tells Timothy that he was ordained for no other purpose than to point men to Him who alone can intercede.

III

'*One God--but no Mediator!*' cries Job.

'*One God--and one Mediator!*' exclaims Paul.

In one respect these two thinkers, standing with a long, long file of centuries between them, are in perfect agreement. They both feel that if there is a God--and only one--no man living can afford to drift into alienation from Him. If there is **no** God, I can live as I list and do as I please; I am answerable to nobody. If there are ***many gods***, I can offend one or two of them without involving myself in uttermost disaster and despair. But if there is ***one*** God, and only one, everything depends upon my relationship with Him. And if I am already estranged from Him, and if there be no Mediator by whose good offices a reconciliation may be effected, then am I of all men most miserable.

'*One God--but no Mediator!*' cried Job in despair.

'*One God--and one Mediator!*' exclaims Paul, in delight.

IV

'*One God--and one Mediator!*'

It is the glory of our humanity that it needs both the one and the other. We need a God and cannot be happy till we find Him. The instinct of adoration is in our blood, and we are ill at ease until we can find One at whose feet we can lay the tribute of our devotion. We need a Mediator, too, and are at our best when we recognize and confess our need of Him. It is, I say, the glory of a man that he can yearn for these two things. The most faithful and intelligent of the beasts feel no desire for either the one or the other. We know how Dr. Davidson died. I said that his conversation with Drumsheugh was his last. I was mistaken. His last conversation was with Skye, his dog. When John, the serving-man, paid his usual visit to the study before he went to bed, the doctor did not hear him enter the room. He was holding converse with Skye, who was seated on a chair, looking very wise and deeply interested.

'Ye're a bonnie beastie, Skye,' exclaimed the doctor, 'for a' thing He made is verra gude. Ye've been true and kind to your master, Skye, and ye 'ill miss him if he leaves ye. Some day ye 'ill die also, and they 'ill bury ye, and I doubt that 'ill be the end o' ye, Skye! Ye never heard o' God, Skye, or the Saviour, for ye're just a puir doggie; but your master is minister of Drumtochty and--a sinner saved by grace!'

Those were his last words. In the morning the doctor was still sitting in his big chair, and Skye was fondly licking a hand that would never again caress him.

Skye, the noblest dog in the world, had no sense of sin and no sense of grace, no need of a God and no need of a Saviour!

Dr. Davidson, Skye's master, is a sinner saved by grace. And it is his sense of sin and his sense of grace, his need of a God and his need of a Saviour, that remove him by whole infinities from the faithful brute on the chair. 'A sinner,' as our fathers used to sing:

A sinner is a sacred thing,   The Holy Ghost hath made him so.

When the soul feels after God, and the heart cries out for a Saviour, it is proof positive of the divinity that dwells within us.

V

'***One God--but no Mediator!***' sighs Job.
'***One God--and one Mediator!***' cries Paul.

None! One! The difference between *none* and *one* is a difference of millions. *None* means nothing, *one* means everything. *None* means failure: *one* means felicity. *None* means despair: *one* means delight. *None* means perdition: *one* means paradise. The difference between '*no Mediator*' and '*one Mediator*' is a difference that can never be worked out by arithmetic.

'***One God***'--and only one!

'***And one Mediator!***'--only one!

But one is enough. It is only in the small things of life that I long for a selection; in the great things of life I only long for satisfaction. When my appetite is sated, and food is almost a matter of indifference to me, I like to be invited to choose between this, that, and the other. But when I am starving, I do not hanker after a choice. I do not want to choose. Put food before me, and I am content. If I am taking a stroll for the mere pleasure of walking, I like to come to a place where several roads meet, and to select the path that seems to be most tempting. But if, weary and travelworn, I am struggling desperately homewards, I do not want to have to choose my path. I dread the place where many roads meet--the place where I may go astray. My felicity lies in simplicity: I want but one road if that road leads home. Robinson Crusoe climbs the hills of his island solitude and shades his eyes with his hand as he sweeps the watery horizon. He is looking for a sail. *One* ship will do: he does not want a fleet. There is but *one* way of salvation for my storm-tossed soul: there is but *one* Name given under heaven among men whereby we must be saved: '***there is one God and one Mediator between God and Men***'--and *one* is ample. The difference between '*no Mediator*' and '*one Mediator*' is a difference that has all eternity within it.

VI

But it is time that we came to close quarters. There are two people in every congregation with whom the minister finds it very difficult to deal. There is the man upon whose conscience sin lies very heavily, and there is the man upon whose soul it sits very lightly.

The *first* of these two perplexing individuals is afraid to approach the Mediator. He feels it to be a kind of presumption. It is difficult to argue with him. It is better to introduce him to Robert Murray McCheyne. McCheyne had the same feeling. 'I am ashamed to go to Christ,' he says. 'I feel, when I have sinned, that it would do no good to go. It seems to be making Christ a Minister of Sin to go straight from the swine-trough to the best robe.' But he came to see that there is no other way, and that all his plausible reasonings were but the folly of his own beclouded heart. 'The weight of my sin,' he writes, 'should act like the weight of a clock; the heavier it is, the faster it makes it go!'

And the *second* of these difficult cases--the man upon whose conscience sin sits so lightly--I shall introduce to Dr. MacLure. As Drumsheugh told Dr. Davidson on that snowy Christmas night, 'if ever there was a man who could have stood on his own feet in the Day of Judgment, it was William MacLure.' Through all his long years in the glen, the old doctor had simply lived for others. As long as he could cure his patients he was content; and he was never happier than in handing the sick child back to its parents or in restoring the wife to the husband who had despaired of her recovery. If ever there was a man who could have stood on his own feet in the Day of Judgment, it was William MacLure. Yet when the old doctor came to the end of his long journey, his soul was feeling after the same thing--a Friend in the Great Court, an Intercessor, a Mediator between God and men!

'We have done our best,' said the old minister, in that last talk with his elder, 'we have done our best, but the less we say about it the better. We need a Friend to say a good word for us in the Great Court.'

'A've thocht that masel,' replied the agonized elder, 'mair than aince. Weelum MacLure was 'ettling aifter the same thing the nicht he slippit awa, an' gin ony man cud hae stude on his ain feet yonder, it was Weelum.'

And for minister and elder and doctor--and me--'*there is one God and one Mediator between God and men, the man Christ Jesus.*'

VII
HENRY MARTYN'S TEXT

I

With Henry Martyn the making of history became a habit, a habit so inveterate that not even death itself could break him of it. He only lived to be thirty-two; but he made vast quantities of history in that meager handful of years. 'His,' says Sir James Stephen, 'is the one heroic name which adorns the annals of the English church from the days of Elizabeth to our own.' And Dr. George Smith, his biographer, boasts that Martyn's life constitutes itself the priceless and perpetual heritage of all English-speaking Christendom, whilst the native churches of India, Arabia, Persia and Anatolia will treasure the thought of it through all time to come. Appropriately enough, Macaulay, who dedicated his brilliant powers to the great task of worthily recording the history that other men had made, composed the epitaph for that lonely Eastern tomb.

Here Martyn lies! In manhood's early bloom   The Christian hero found a Pagan tomb: Religion, sorrowing o'er her favorite son,   Points to the glorious trophies which he won.   Eternal trophies, not with slaughter red,   Not stained with tears by hopeless captives shed;   But trophies of the Cross. For that dear Name Through every form of danger, death and shame,   Onward he journeyed to a happier shore,   Where danger, death and shame are known no more.

For more than a hundred years the bones of Henry Martyn have reposed in that far-off Oriental sepulcher; but, as though he had never heard of his own decease, he goes on making history still. Henry Martyn died seven years before George Eliot was born, and they had very little in common. But, in the novel which Dr. Marcus

Dods described as 'one of the greatest religious books ever written,' George Eliot makes the spiritual crisis in the experience of her storm-beaten and distracted heroine to turn on the perusal of the *Life of Henry Martyn*. When Janet Dempster, clad only in her thin nightdress, was driven at dead of night from her husband's home, she took refuge with good old Mrs. Pettifer, and fell into a stupor of utter misery and black despair. Nothing seemed to rouse her. It chanced, however, that Mrs. Pettifer was a subscriber of the Paddiford Lending Library. From that village treasure-trove she had borrowed the biography that was lying on the table when, like a hunted deer, poor Janet took shelter in her home. After a day or two, Janet picked up the book, dipped into it, and at length 'became so arrested by that pathetic missionary story that she could not leave it alone.' It broke the spell of her stupor, gave her a new hold upon life, awoke her dormant energy, and moved her to renewed action.

'I must go,' she said. 'I feel I must be doing something for someone; I must not be a mere useless log any longer. I've been reading about that wonderful Henry Martyn wearing himself out for *other people*, and I sit thinking of nothing but *myself*! I must go! Good-bye!'

And, like a frightened dove that, having been driven to shelter by a hawk, recovers from its terror and again takes wing, off she went! Janet Dempster is all the more real because she is unreal. She is all the more a substance because she is only a shadow. She is all the more symbolic and typical because she appears, not in history, but in fiction. If I had found her in the realm of biography, I might have regarded hers as an isolated and exceptional case. But, since I have found her in the realm of romance, I can only regard her--as her creator intended me to regard her--as a great representative character. She represents all those thousands of people upon whom the heroic record of Henry Martyn's brief career has acted as a stimulant and a tonic. She represents all those thousands of people through whom Henry Martyn is making history.

II

The Gospels tell of a certain man who was *borne of four* to the feet of Jesus.

I know his name and I know the names of the four who brought him. The man's name was Henry Martyn, and the quartet consisted of a father, a sister, an author and a minister. Each had a hand in the gracious work, and each in a different way. The father did his part accidentally, indirectly, unconsciously; the sister did her part designedly, deliberately, and of set purpose. The author and the minister did their parts in the ordinary pursuit of their vocations; but the ***author*** did his part impersonally and indirectly, whilst the ***minister*** did his part personally and face to face. The author's shaft was from a bow drawn at a venture; the minister's was carefully aimed. He set himself to win the young student in his congregation, and he lived to rejoice unfeignedly in his success. Let me introduce each of the four.

The Father bore his Corner. Before Henry Martyn left England, he was one of the most brilliant students in the country, Senior Wrangler of his University, and the proud holder of scholarships and fellowships. But, in his earlier days, he failed at one or two examinations, and, in his mortification, heaped the blame upon his father. In one of these fits of passion, he bounced out of the elder man's presence--never to enter it again. Before he could return and express contrition, the father suddenly died. Henry's remorse was pitiful to see. His heart was filled with grief and his eyes swollen with tears. But that torrent of tears so cleansed those eyes that he was able to see, as he had never seen before, into the abysmal depths of his own heart. He was astonished at the baseness and depravity he found there. Years afterwards he writes with emotion of the distressing discovery that he then made. 'I do not remember a time,' he says, 'in which the wickedness of my heart rose to a greater height than it did then. The consummate selfishness and exquisite instability of my mind were displayed in rage, malice and envy; in pride, vain-glory and contempt for all about me; and in the harsh language which I used to my sister and even to my father. Oh, what an example of patience and mildness was he! I love to think of his excellent qualities; and it is the anguish of my heart that I could ever have been base enough and wicked enough to have pained him. O my God, why is not my heart doubly-agonized at the remembrance of all my great transgressions?' So poor John Martyn, lying silent in his grave, entered into that felicity which, in one of her short poems, Miss Susan Best has so touchingly depicted. 'When I was laid in my coffin,' she makes a dead man say,

When I was laid in my coffin,
  Quite done with Time and its fears,
My son came and stood beside me--
  He hadn't been home for years;
And right on my face came dripping
  The scald of his salty tears;
And I was glad to know his breast
  Had turned at last to the old home nest,
That I said to myself in an underbreath:
'This is the recompense of death.'

The Sister bore her Corner. In his letters to her he opens all his heart. He is sometimes angry with her because, when he expected her to show delight in his academic triumphs, she only exhibits an earnest solicitude for his spiritual well-being. But, in his better moments, he forgave her. 'What a blessing it is for me,' he writes to her in his twentieth year, 'what a blessing it is for me that I have such a sister as you, who have been so instrumental in keeping me in the right way.' And, later on, he delights her by telling her that he 'has begun to attend more diligently to the words of the Saviour and to devour them with delight.'

The Author bore his Corner. It was just about a hundred years after the birth of Philip Doddridge, and just about fifty years after his death, that his book, ***The Rise and Progress of Religion in the Soul***, fell into the hands of Henry Martyn. Twenty years earlier it had opened the eyes of William Wilberforce and led him to repentance. Doddridge's powerful sentences fell upon the proud soul of Henry Martyn like the lashes of a scourge. He resented them; he writhed under their condemnation; but they revealed to him the desperate need of his heart, and he could not shake from him the alarm which they excited.

The Minister bore his Corner. No preacher in England was better fitted to appeal to the mind of Martyn, at this critical stage of his career, than was the Rev. Charles Simeon, the Vicar of Trinity Church, Cambridge. In his concern, the young collegian found himself strangely attracted to the services at Trinity; and he gradually acquired, as he confessed to his sister, more knowledge in divine things. He made the acquaintance, and won the friendship, of Mr. Simeon, and confided in him without reserve. 'I now experienced,' he says, 'a real pleasure in religion, being more deeply convinced of sin than before, more earnest in fleeing to Jesus for refuge, and more desirous for the renewal of my nature.' The profit was mutual. For, many years after Henry Martyn's departure and death, Mr. Simeon kept in his study a portrait of the young student, and he used to say that he could never look into that face but it seemed to say to him, 'Be earnest! Be earnest!'

And so, to repeat the language of the Gospel, '***there came unto Jesus one that was borne of four***,' and his name was Henry Martyn.

III

I cannot discover that, up to this point, any one text had played a conspicuous part in precipitating the crisis which transfigured his life. But, after this, I find one sentence repeatedly on his lips. During a journey a man is often too engrossed with the perplexities of the immediate present to be able to review the path as a whole. But, when he looks back, he surveys the entire landscape in grateful retrospect, and is astonished at the multiplicity and variety of the perils that he has escaped. Henry Martyn had some such feeling. When, at the age of twenty-two, he entered the ministry, he was amazed at the greatness of the grace that had made such hallowed privileges and sacred duties possible to him. Even in his first sermon, we are told, he preached with a fervor of spirit and an earnestness of manner that deeply impressed the congregation.

He preached as one who ne'er should preach again,   And as a dying man to dying men.

'For,' he wrote, '***I am but a brand plucked from the burning.***'

Again, when the needs of the world pressed like an intolerable burden upon his spirit, the same thought decided his course. On the ***one*** hand, he saw a world lying in darkness and crying for the light. On the ***other*** hand, he saw all those sweet and sacred ties that bound him to his native land--his devoted people, his admiring friends, and, hardest tie of all to break, the lady whom he had fondly hoped to make his bride. Here, on the ***one*** hand, stood comfort, popularity, success and love! And here, on the **other**, stood cruel hardship, endless difficulties, constant loneliness, and an early grave! 'But how,' he writes, 'can I hesitate? *I am but a brand plucked from the burning!'*

A brand in peril of sharing the general destruction!
A brand seen, and prized, and rescued!
A brand at whose blaze other flames might be lit!
A brand plucked from the burning!

IV

'*Is not this a brand plucked from the burning?*'--it was John Wesley's text. To the end of his days John Wesley preserved the picture of the fire at the old rectory, the fire from which he, as a child of six, was only rescued in the nick of time. And, underneath the picture, John Wesley had written with his own hand the words: '***Is not this a brand plucked from the burning?***'

'*Is not this a brand plucked from the burning?*'--it was John Fletcher's text. John Wesley thought John Fletcher, the Vicar of Madeley, the holiest man then living. 'I have known him intimately for thirty years,' says Mr. Wesley. 'In my eighty years I have met many excellent men; but I have never met his equal, nor do I expect to find such another on this side of eternity.' From what source did that perennial stream of piety spring? 'When I saw that all my endeavors availed nothing,' says Mr. Fletcher, in describing his conversion, 'I almost gave up hope. But, I thought, Christ died for ***all***; therefore He died for ***me***. He died to pluck such sinners as I am ***as brands from the burning***! I felt my helplessness and lay at the feet of Christ. I cried, coldly, yet, I believe, sincerely, "Save me, Lord, ***as a brand snatched out of the fire***! Stretch forth Thine almighty arm and save Thy lost creature by free, unmerited grace!"'

'*Is not this a brand plucked from the burning?*'--it was Thomas Olivers' text. Thomas Olivers was one of Wesley's veterans, the author of the well-known hymn, 'The God of Abraham praise.' He went one day to hear George Whitefield preach. The text was, '***Is not this a brand plucked from the burning?***' 'When the sermon began,' he says, 'I was certainly a dreadful enemy to God and to all that is good, and one of the most profligate and abandoned young men living; but, by the time it was ended, I was become a new creature. For, in the first place, I was deeply convinced of the great goodness of God towards me in all my life; particularly in that He had given His Son to die for me. I had also a far clearer view of all my sins, particularly my base ingratitude towards Him. These discoveries quite broke my heart and caused showers of tears to trickle down my cheeks. I was likewise filled with an utter abhorrence of my evil ways, and was much ashamed that I had ever walked in them. And, as my heart was thus turned from all that is evil, so it was powerfully inclined to all that is good. It is not easy to express what strong desires I felt for God and His service; and what resolutions I made to seek Him and serve Him in the future. In consequence of this, I broke off all my evil practices, and forsook all my wicked and foolish companions without delay. I gave myself up to God and His service with my whole heart. Oh, what reason have I to say, "*Is not this a brand plucked from the burning?*"'

'*Is not this a brand plucked from the burning?*'--it was Stephen Grellet's text. Writing of his conversion, he says that 'the awfulness of that day of God's visitation can never cease to be remembered by me with peculiar gratitude as long as I possess my mental faculties. I am *as a brand plucked from the burning*; I have been rescued from the brink of a horrible pit!'

V

And it was Henry Martyn's text! '*Is not this*,' he cried, as he entered the ministry, and again as he entered the mission field, '*is not this a brand plucked from the burning?*'

A brand that might have perished in the general destruction!
A brand seen, and prized, and rescued!
A brand at whose blaze other flames might be lit!
A brand plucked from the burning!

'Oh, let me burn out for my God!' he cries, still thinking of the brand plucked from the flames. He plunges, like a blazing torch, into the darkness of India, of Persia and of Turkey. He leaves the peoples whom he has evangelized the Scriptures in their own tongues. Seven short years after he left England, he dies all alone on a foreign strand. 'No kinsman is near to watch his last look or receive his last words. No friend stands by his couch to whisper comforting words, to close his eyes or wipe the death-sweat from his brow.' In the article of death, he is alone with his Lord. The brand plucked from the blaze has soon burned out. But what does it matter? At its ardent flame a thousand other torches have been ignited; and the lands that sat so long in darkness have welcomed the coming of a wondrous light!

VIII
MICHAEL TREVANION'S TEXT

I

Michael Trevanion misunderstood Paul: that was the trouble. Michael, so Mark Rutherford tells us, was a Puritan of the Puritans, silent, stern, unbending. Between his wife and himself no sympathy existed. They had two children--a boy and a girl. The girl was in every way her mother's child: the boy was the image of his father. Michael made a companion of his son; took him into his own workshop; and promised himself that, come what might, Robert should grow up to walk in his father's footsteps. All went well until Robert Trevanion met Susan Shipton. Susan was one of the beauties of that Cornish village. She had--what were not common in Cornwall--light flaxen hair, blue eyes, and a rosy face, somewhat inclined to be plump. The Shiptons lay completely outside Michael's circle. They were mere formalists in religion, fond of pleasure; and Susan especially was much given to gaiety. She went to picnics and dances; rowed herself about the bay with her friends; and sauntered round the town with her father and mother on Sunday afternoons. She was fond of bathing, too, and was a good swimmer. Michael hardly knew how to put his objection in words, but he nevertheless had a horror of women who could swim. It seemed to him an ungodly accomplishment. He did not believe for a moment that Paul would have sanctioned it. That settled it for Michael. For Michael had unbounded faith in the judgment of Paul; and the tragedy of his life lay in the fact that, on one important occasion, he misunderstood his oracle.

One summer's morning, Robert saved Susan from drowning. She had forgotten the swirl of water caused by the rush of the river into the bay, and had swum into the danger zone. In three minutes Robert was at her side, had gripped her by the bathing dress at the back of her neck, and had brought her into safer water. From that moment the two were often together; and, one afternoon, Michael came suddenly upon them and guessed their secret. It nearly broke his heart. In Robert's attachment to Susan he saw--or thought he saw--the end of all his hopes. 'He remembered what his own married life had been; he always trusted that Robert would have a wife who would be a help to him, and he felt sure that this girl Shipton, with her pretty face and blue eyes, had no brains. To think that his boy should repeat the same inexplicable blunder, that he would never hear from his wife's lips one serious word! What would she be if trouble came upon him? She was not a child of God. He did not know that she ever sought the Lord. She went to church once a day and read her prayers, and that was all. She was not one of the chosen; she might corrupt Robert and he might fall away and so commit the sin against the Holy Ghost. He went to his room, and, shutting the door, wept bitter tears. 'O my son, Absalom,' he cried, 'my son, my son Absalom! Would God I had died for thee, O Absalom, my son, my son!'

It was in these desperate straits that poor Michael consulted Paul--and misunderstood him. It was a Sunday night. Michael picked up the Bible and turned to the Epistle to the Romans. It was his favorite epistle. He read the ninth chapter. The third verse startled him. '***I could wish that myself were accursed from Christ for my brethren, my kinsmen according to the flesh.*** ' Nobody need wonder that the words strangely affected him. In his ***Table Talk***, Coleridge says that when he read this passage to a friend of his, a Jew at Ramsgate, the old man burst into tears. 'Any Jew of sensibility,' the poet adds, 'must be deeply impressed by it.' Michael Trevanion read the throbbing words again. '***I could wish that myself were accursed from Christ for my brethren, my kinsmen according to the flesh.***'

He laid down the Book. 'What did Paul mean? What **could** he mean save that he was willing to be damned to save those whom he loved? And why not? Why should not a man be willing to be damned for others? Damnation! It is awful, horrible. Millions of years, with no relief, with no light from the Most High, and in subjection to His enemy! "And yet, if it is to save--if it is to save Robert," thought Michael, "God give me strength--I could endure it. Did not the Son Himself venture to risk the wrath of the Father that He might redeem man? What am I? What is my poor self?" And Michael determined that night that neither his life in this world nor in the next, if he could rescue his child, should be of any account.'

So far Michael and Paul were of one mind. Now for the divergence! Now for the misunderstanding! Michael questioned himself and his oracle further. 'What could Paul mean exactly? God could not curse him *if he did no wrong*. He could only mean that he was willing *to sin*, and be punished, provided Israel might live. It was lawful then to *tell a lie or perpetrate any evil deed* in order to protect his child.' Michael therefore took his resolution. He hinted to Robert that Susan's history was besmirched with shame. He left on his desk--where he knew Robert would see it--a fragment of an old letter referring to the downfall of another girl named Susan. Michael knew that he was telling and acting a lie, a terrible and unpardonable lie. He firmly believed that, in telling that dreadful lie, he was damning his soul to all eternity. But in damning his own soul--so he thought--he was saving his son's. And that, after all, was the lesson that Paul had taught him.

The rest of the story does not immediately concern us. Robert, on seeing the documentary proof of Susan's shame, ran away from home. Michael, overwhelmed with wretchedness, attempted to drown himself in the swirl at the mouth of the river. Of what value was life to him, now that his soul was everlastingly lost? He awoke to find himself on the bank, with Susan bending over him and kissing him. He soon discovered that there was more sense in Susan's head, and more grace in her heart, than he had for one moment imagined. He set out after his son; found him; and died in making his great and humiliating confession. He had meant well, but he had misunderstood. He had misunderstood Paul.

II

Michael made two mistakes, and they were grave and tragic and fatal mistakes.

He thought that good fruit could be produced from an evil tree. There are times when it looks possible. But it is always an illusion. When I see Michael Trevanion in the hour of his great temptation, I wish I could introduce him to

Jeanie Deans. For, in *The Heart of Midlothian*, Sir Walter Scott has outlined a very similar situation. Poor Jeanie was tempted to save her wayward sister by a lie. It was a very little lie, a mere glossing over of the truth. The slightest deviation from actual veracity, and her sister's life, which was dearer to her than her own, would be saved from the scaffold, and her family honor would be vindicated. But Jeanie could not, and would not, believe that there could be salvation in a lie. With her gentle heart reproaching her, but with her conscience applauding her, she told the truth, the whole truth, and nothing but the truth. And then she set out for London. Along the great white road she trudged, until her feet were bleeding and her exhausted form could scarcely drag itself along the dreadful miles. But on she pressed, until she saw the lights of London town; and still on, overcoming every barrier, until she stood before the Queen. And then she pleaded, as no mere advocate could plead, for Effie. With what passion, what entreaties, what tears did she besiege the throne! And, before the tempest of her grief and eloquence, the Queen yielded completely and gave her her sister's life. To Jeanie Deans and to Michael Trevanion there came the same terrible ordeal; but Jeanie stood where Michael fell. That was the *first* of his two mistakes.

The *second* was that **he thought that spiritual results could be engineered**. He fancied that souls could be saved by wire-pulling.

'Robert,' he said, on the day of his death and of his bitter confession, 'Robert, I have sinned, although it was for the Lord's sake, and He has rebuked me. I thought to take upon myself the direction of His affairs; but He is wiser than I. I believed I was sure of His will, but I was mistaken. He knows that what I did, I did for the love of your soul, my child; but I was grievously wrong.'

'The father,' says Mark Rutherford, 'humbled himself before the son, but in his humiliation became majestic; and, in after years, when he was dead and gone, there was no scene in the long intercourse with him which lived with a brighter and fairer light in the son's memory.'

III

And so Michael Trevanion sinned and suffered for his sin! For my part, I have no stones to cast at him. I would rather sit at his feet and learn the golden lesson of his life. For love--and especially the love of an earnest man for another's soul--covers a multitude of sins. There come to all of us mountain moments, moments in which we stand on the higher altitudes and catch a glimpse of the unutterable preciousness of a human soul. But we are disobedient to the heavenly vision. We are like Augustine Saint Clare in **Uncle Tom's Cabin**. He could never forget, he said, the words with which his mother impressed upon him the dignity and worth of the souls of the slaves. Those passionate sentences of hers seemed to have burnt themselves into his brain. 'I have looked into her face with solemn awe,' he told Miss Ophelia, 'when she pointed to the stars in the evening and said to me, "See there, Auguste! the poorest, meanest soul on our place will be living when all those stars are gone for ever--will live as long as God lives!"'

'Then why don't you free your slaves?' asked Miss Ophelia, with a woman's practical and incisive logic.

'I'm not equal to that!' Saint Clare replied; and he confessed that, through having proved recreant to the ideals that had once so clearly presented themselves, he was not the man that he might have been.

'I'm not equal to that!' said Augustine Saint Clare.

But Michael Trevanion *was* equal to that--and to a great deal more. He saw the value of his son's soul, and he was willing to be shut out of heaven for ever and ever if only Robert could be eternally saved! 'My witness is above,' says Samuel Rutherford, in his **Second Letter to his Parishioners**, 'my witness is above that your heaven would be two heavens to me, and the salvation of you all as two salvations to me. I would agree to a suspension and a postponement of my heaven for many hundreds of years if ye could so be assured of a lodging in the Father's house.' Michael Trevanion's behavior--mistaken as it was--proved that he was willing to make an even greater sacrifice if, by so doing, he could compass the salvation of his son.

IV

It is at this point that Michael Trevanion falls into line with the great masters.

Since the apostolic days we have had two conspicuously successful evangelists--John Wesley and Mr. Spurgeon. The secret of their success is so obvious that he who runs may read. I turn to my edition of John Wesley's *Journal*, and at the end I find a tribute like this: 'The great purpose of his life was doing good. For this he relinquished all honor and preferment; to this he dedicated all his powers of body and mind; at all times and in all places, in season and out of season, by gentleness, by terror, by argument, by persuasion, by reason, by interest, by every motive and every inducement, he strove, with unwearied assiduity, to turn men from the error of their ways and awaken them to virtue and religion. To the bed of sickness or the couch of prosperity; to the prison or the hospital; to the house of mourning or the house of feasting, wherever there was a friend to serve or a soul to save, he readily repaired. He thought no office too humiliating, no condescension too low, no undertaking too arduous, to reclaim the meanest of God's offspring. ***The souls of all men were equally precious in his sight and the value of an immortal creature beyond all estimation.***'

In relation to Mr. Spurgeon, we cannot do better than place ourselves under Mr. W. Y. Fullerton's direction. Mr. Fullerton knew Mr. Spurgeon intimately, and the standard biography of the great preacher is from his pen. Mr. Fullerton devotes a good deal of his space to an inquiry as to the sources of Mr. Spurgeon's power and authority. It is an elusive and difficult question. It is admitted that there is scarcely one respect in which Mr. Spurgeon's powers were really transcendent. He had a fine voice; but others had finer ones. He was eloquent; but others were no less so. He used to say that his success was due, not to his preaching of the Gospel, but to the Gospel that he preached. Obviously, however, this is beside the mark, for he himself would not have been so uncharitable as to deny that others preached the same Gospel and yet met with no corresponding success. The truth probably is that, although he attained to super-excellence at no point, he was really great at many. And, behind this extraordinary combination of remarkable, though not transcendent, powers was an intense conviction, a deadly earnestness, a consuming passion, that made second-rate qualities sublime. The most revealing paragraph in the book occurs towards the end. It is a quotation from Mr. Spurgeon himself. 'Leaving home early in the morning,' he says, 'I went to the vestry and sat there all day long, seeing those who had been brought to Christ by the preaching of the Word. Their stories were so interesting to me that the hours flew by without my noticing how fast they were going. I had seen numbers of persons during the day, one after the other; and I was so delighted with the tales of divine mercy they had to tell me, and the wonders of grace God wrought in them, that I did not notice how the time passed. At seven o'clock we had our prayer meeting. I went in to it. After that came the church meeting. A little before ten I felt faint, and I began to think at what hour I had eaten my dinner, and I then for the first time remembered that *I had not had any*! I never thought of it. I never even felt hungry, because God had made me so glad!' Mr. Spurgeon lived that he might save men. He thought of nothing else. From his first sermon at Waterbeach to his last at Mentone, the conversion of sinners was the dream of all his days. That master-passion glorified the whole man, and threw a grandeur about the common details of every day. He would cheerfully have thrown away his soul to save the souls of others.

It is along this road that the Church has always marched to her most splendid triumphs. Why did the Roman Empire so swiftly capitulate to the claims of Christ? Lecky discusses that question in his ***History of European Morals***. And he answers it by saying that the conquest was achieved by the new spirit which Christ had introduced. The idea of a Saviour who could weep at the sepulcher of His friend; and be touched by a sense of His people's infirmities, was a novelty to that old pagan world. And when the early Christians showed themselves willing to endure any suffering, or bear any loss, if, by so doing, they might win their friends, their sincerity and devotion proved irresistible.

V

But Michael Trevanion must lead us higher yet. For what Michael Trevanion learned from Paul, Paul himself had learned from an infinitely greater. Let us trace it back!

'Let me be damned to all eternity that my boy may be saved!' cries Michael Trevanion, sitting at the feet of Paul, but misunderstanding his teacher.

'*I could wish that myself were accursed from Christ for my brethren, my kinsmen according to the flesh*,' exclaims Paul, sitting at the feet of One who not only *wished* to be accursed, but *entered into* the impenetrable darkness of that dreadful anathema.

'*My God, my God, why hast Thou forsaken Me?*' He cried from that depth of dereliction. 'In that awful hour,' said Rabbi Duncan, addressing his students, 'in that awful hour ***He took our damnation, and He took it lovingly!*** When, with reverent hearts and bated breath, we peer down into the fathomless deeps that such a saying opens to us, we catch a glimpse of the inexpressible value which heaven sets upon the souls of men. And, when Michael Trevanion has led us to such inaccessible heights and to such unutterable depths as these, we can very well afford to say Good-bye to him.

IX
HUDSON TAYLOR'S TEXT

I

The day on which James Hudson Taylor--then a boy in his teens--found himself confronted by that tremendous text was, as he himself testified in old age, 'a day that he could never forget.' It is a day that China can never forget; a day that the world can never forget. It was a holiday; everybody was away from home; and the boy found time hanging heavily upon his hands. In an aimless way he wandered, during the afternoon, into his father's library, and poked about among the shelves. 'I tried,' he says, 'to find some book with which to while away the leaden hours. Nothing attracting me, I turned over a basket of pamphlets and selected from among them a tract that looked interesting. I knew that it would have a story at the commencement and a moral at the close; but I promised myself that I would enjoy the story and leave the rest. It would be easy to put away the tract as soon as it should seem prosy.' He scampers off to the stable-loft, throws himself on the hay, and plunges into the book. He is captivated by the narrative, and finds it impossible to drop the book when the story comes to an end. He reads on and on. He is rewarded by one great golden word whose significance he has never before discovered: '*The Finished Work of Christ!*' The theme entrances him; and at last he only rises from his bed in the soft hay that he may kneel on the hard floor of the loft and surrender his young life to the Saviour who had surrendered everything for him. If, he asked himself, as he lay upon the hay, if the whole work was finished, and the whole debt paid upon the Cross, what is there left for me to do? 'And then,' he tells us, 'there dawned upon me the joyous conviction that there was nothing in the world to be done but to fall upon my knees, accept the Saviour and praise Him for evermore.'

'*It is finished!*'

'*When Jesus, therefore, had received the vinegar he said, "It is finished!" and He bowed His head and gave up the ghost.*'

'*Then there dawned upon me the joyous conviction that, since the whole work was finished and the whole debt paid upon the Cross, there was nothing for me to do but to fall upon my knees, accept the Saviour and praise Him for evermore!*'

II

'*It is finished!*'

It is really only one word: the greatest word ever uttered; we must examine it for a moment as a lapidary examines under a powerful glass a rare and costly gem.

It was a *farmer's* word. When, into his herd, there was born an animal so beautiful and shapely that it seemed absolutely destitute of faults and defects, the farmer gazed upon the creature with proud, delighted eyes. '*Tetelestai!*' he said, '*tetelestai!*'

It was an *artist's* word. When the painter or the sculptor had put the last finishing touches to the vivid landscape or the marble bust, he would stand back a few feet to admire his masterpiece, and, seeing in it nothing that called for correction or improvement, would murmur fondly, '*Tetelestai! tetelestai!*'

It was a *priestly* word. When some devout worshiper, overflowing with gratitude for mercies shown him, brought to the temple a lamb without spot or blemish, the pride of the whole flock, the priest, more accustomed to seeing the blind and defective animals led to the altar, would look admiringly upon the pretty creature. '*Tetelestai!*' he would say, '*tetelestai!*'

And when, in the fullness of time, the Lamb of God offered Himself on the altar of the ages, He rejoiced with a joy so triumphant that it bore down all His anguish before it. The sacrifice was stainless, perfect, finished! '***He cried with a loud***

voice Tetelestai! and gave up the ghost.'

This divine self-satisfaction appears only twice, once in each Testament. When He completed the work of Creation, He looked upon it and said that it was very good; when He completed the work of Redemption He cried with a loud voice ***Tetelestai***! It means exactly the same thing.

III

The joy of finishing and of finishing well! How passionately good men have coveted for themselves that ecstasy! I think of those pathetic entries in Livingstone's journal. 'Oh, to finish my work!' he writes again and again. He is haunted by the vision of the unseen waters, the fountains of the Nile. Will he live to discover them? 'Oh, to finish!' he cries; 'if only I could finish my work!' I think of Henry Buckle, the author of the ***History of Civilization***. He is overtaken by fever at Nazareth and dies at Damascus. In his delirium he raves continually about his book, his still unfinished book. 'Oh, to finish my book!' And with the words 'My book! my book!' upon his burning lips, his spirit slips away. I think of Henry Martyn sitting amidst the delicious and fragrant shades of a Persian garden, weeping at having to leave the work that he seemed to have only just begun. I think of Dore taking a sad farewell of his unfinished ***Vale of Tears***; of Dickens tearing himself from the manuscript that he knew would never be completed; of Macaulay looking with wistful and longing eyes at the ***History*** and ***The Armada*** that must for ever stand as 'fragments'; and of a host besides. Life is often represented by a broken column in the church-yard. Men long, but long in vain, for the priceless privilege of finishing their work.

IV

The joy of finishing and of finishing well! There is no joy on earth comparable to this. Who is there that has not read a dozen times the immortal postscript that Gibbon added to his ***Decline and Fall?*** He describes the tumult of emotion with which, after twenty years of closest application, he wrote the last line of the last chapter of the last volume of his masterpiece. It was a glorious summer's night at Lausanne. 'After laying down my pen,' he says, 'I took several turns in a covered walk of acacias which commands a prospect of the country, the lake and the mountains. The air was temperate, the sky was serene, the silver orb of the moon was reflected from the waters, and all nature was silent.' It was the greatest moment of his life. We recall, too, the similar experience of Sir Archibald Alison. 'As I approached the closing sentence of my **History of the Empire**,' he says, 'I went up to Mrs. Alison to call her down to witness the conclusion, and she saw the last words of the work written, and signed her name on the margin. It would be affectation to conceal the deep emotion that I felt at this event.' Or think of the last hours of Venerable Bede. Living away back in the early dawn of our English story--twelve centuries ago--the old man had set himself to translate the Gospel of John into our native speech. Cuthbert, one of his young disciples, has bequeathed to us the touching record. As the work approached completion, he says, death drew on apace. The aged scholar was racked with pain; sleep forsook him; he could scarcely breathe. The young man who wrote at his dictation implored him to desist. But he would not rest. They came at length to the final chapter; could he possibly live till it was done?

'And now, dear master,' exclaimed the young scribe tremblingly, 'only one sentence remains!' He read the words and the sinking man feebly recited the English equivalents.

'It is finished, dear master!' cried the youth excitedly.

'Ay, *it is finished*!' echoed the dying saint; 'lift me up, place me at that window of my cell at which I have so often prayed to God. Now glory be to the Father and to the Son and to the Holy Ghost!' And, with these triumphant words, the beautiful spirit passed to its rest and its reward.

V

In his own narrative of his conversion, Hudson Taylor quotes James Proctor's well-known hymn--the hymn that, in one of his essays, Froude criticizes so severely:

Nothing either great or small,
  Nothing, sinner, no;   Jesus did it, did it all,
  Long, long ago.
'*It is Finished!*' yes, indeed,
  Finished every jot;   Sinner, this is all you need;
  Tell me, is it not?
Cast your deadly doing down,
  Down at Jesus' feet;
Stand in Him, in Him alone,
  Gloriously complete.

Froude maintains that these verses are immoral. It is only by 'doing,' he argues, that the work of the world can ever get done. And if you describe 'doing' as 'deadly' you set a premium upon indolence and lessen the probabilities of attainment. The best answer to Froude's plausible contention is the **Life of Hudson Taylor**. Hudson Taylor became convinced, as a boy, that 'the whole work was finished and the whole debt paid.' 'There is nothing for me to do,' he says, 'but to fall down on my knees and accept the Saviour.' The chapter in his biography that tells of this spiritual crisis is entitled '**The Finished Work of Christ**,' and it is headed by the quotation:

Upon a life I did not live,
  Upon a death I did not die,
Another's life, Another's death
  I stake my whole eternity.

And, as I have said, the very words that Froude so bitterly condemns are quoted by Hudson Taylor as a reflection of his own experience. And the result? The result is that Hudson Taylor became one of the most prodigious toilers of all time. So far from his trust in '**the Finished Work of Christ**' inclining him to indolence, he felt that he must toil most terribly to make so perfect a Saviour known to the whole wide world. There lies on my desk a Birthday Book which I very highly value. It was given me at the docks by Mr. Thomas Spurgeon as I was leaving England. If you open it at the twenty-first of May you will find these words: '**"Simply to Thy**

Cross I cling" is but half of the Gospel. No one is really clinging to the Cross who is not at the same time faithfully following Christ and doing whatsoever He commands*'; and against those words of Dr. J. R. Miller's in my Birthday Book, you may see the autograph of *J. Hudson Taylor*. He was our guest at the Mosgiel Manse when he set his signature to those striking and significant sentences.

VI

'We Build Like Giants; we Finish Like Jewelers!'--so the old Egyptians wrote over the portals of their palaces and temples. I like to think that the most gigantic task ever attempted on this planet--the work of the world's redemption--was finished with a precision and a nicety that no jeweler could rival.

'*It is finished!*' He cried from the Cross.

'*Tetelestai! Tetelestai!*'

When He looked upon His work in Creation and saw that it was good, He placed it beyond the power of man to improve upon it.

> To gild refined gold, to paint the lily,
> To throw a perfume on the violet,
> To smooth the ice, or add another hue
> Unto the rainbow, or with taper-light
> To seek the beauteous eye of heaven to garnish,
>   Is wasteful and ridiculous excess.

And, similarly, when He looked upon His work in Redemption and cried triumphantly '*Tetelestai,*' He placed it beyond the power of any man to add to it.

There are times when any addition is a subtraction. Some years ago, White House at Washington--the residence of the American Presidents--was in the hands of the painters and decorators. Two large entrance doors had been painted to represent black walnut. The contractor ordered his men to scrape and clean them in readiness for repainting, and they set to work. But when their knives penetrated to the solid timber, they discovered to their astonishment that it was heavy mahogany of a most exquisite natural grain! The work of that earlier decorator, so far from adding to the beauty of the timber, had only served to conceal its essential and inherent glory. It is easy enough to add to the wonders of Creation or of Redemption; but you can never add without subtracting. '***It is finished!***'

VII

Many years ago, Ebenezer Wooton, an earnest but eccentric evangelist, was conducting a series of summer evening services on the village green at Lidford Brook. The last meeting had been held; the crowd was melting slowly away; and the evangelist was engaged in taking down the marquee. All at once a young fellow approached him and asked, casually rather than earnestly, 'Mr. Wooton, what must *I* do to be saved?' The preacher took the measure of his man.

'Too late!' he said, in a matter of fact kind of way, glancing up from a somewhat obstinate tent-peg with which he was struggling. 'Too late, my friend, too late!' The young fellow was startled.

'Oh, don't say that, Mr. Wooton!' he pleaded, a new note coming into his voice. 'Surely it isn't too late just because the meetings are over?'

'Yes, my friend,' exclaimed the evangelist, dropping the cord in his hand, straightening himself up, and looking right into the face of his questioner, 'it's too late! You want to know what you must *do* to be saved, and I tell you that you're hundreds of years too late! The work of salvation is done, completed, ***finished***! It was finished on the Cross; Jesus said so with the last breath that He drew! What more do you want?'

And, then and there, it dawned upon the now earnest inquirer on the village green as, at about the same time, it dawned upon young Hudson Taylor in the hayloft, that '***since the whole work was finished and the whole debt paid upon the Cross, there was nothing for him to do but to fall upon his knees and accept the Saviour.***' And there, under the elms, the sentinel stars witnessing the great transaction, he kneeled in glad thanksgiving and rested his soul for time and for eternity on '***the Finished Work of Christ***.'

VIII

'The Finished Work of Christ!'
'Tetelestai! Tetelestai!'
'It is finished!'

It is not a sigh of relief at having reached the end of things. It is the unutterable joy of the artist who, putting the last touches to the picture that has engrossed him for so long, sees in it the realization of all his dreams and can nowhere find room for improvement. Only once in the world's history did a finishing touch bring a work to absolute perfection; and on that day of days a single flaw would have shattered the hope of the ages.

X
RODNEY STEELE'S TEXT
I

As soon,' Dr. Chalmers used to say, 'as soon as a man comes to understand that ***GOD IS LOVE***, he is infallibly converted.' Mrs. Florence L. Barclay wrote a book to show how Rodney Steele made that momentous and transfiguring discovery. Rodney Steele--the hero of ***The Wall of Partition***--was a great traveler and a brilliant author. He had wandered through India, Africa, Australia, Egypt, China and Japan, and had written a novel colored with the local tints of each of the countries he had visited. He was tall, strong, handsome, bronzed by many suns, and--largely as a result of his literary successes--immensely rich. But he was soured. Years ago he loved a beautiful girl. But an unscrupulous and designing woman had gained his sweetheart's confidence and had poisoned her heart by pouring into her ear the most abominable scandals concerning him. She had returned his letters; and he, in the vain hope of being able to forget, had abandoned himself to travel and to literature. But, on whatever seas he sailed, and on whatever shores he wandered, he nursed in his heart a dreadful hate--a hate of the woman who had so cruelly intervened. And, cherishing that hate, his heart became hard and bitter and sour. He lost faith in love, in womanhood, in God, in everything. And his books reflected the cynicism of his soul. This is Rodney Steele as the story opens. The boat-train moves into Charing Cross, and, after an absence of ten years, he finds himself once more in London.

II

Many years ago, when our grandmothers were girls, they devoted their spare moments to the making of bookmarkers; and on the marker, in colored silk, they embroidered the letters GOD IS LOVE. Dr. Handley Moule, Bishop of Durham, made effective use of such a bookmarker when he visited West Stanley immediately after the terrible colliery disaster there. He motored up to the scene of the catastrophe and addressed the crowd at the pit's mouth. Many of those present were the relatives of the entombed miners. 'It is very difficult,' he said, 'for us to understand why God should let such an awful disaster happen, but we know Him, and trust Him, and all will be right. I have at home,' the Bishop continued, 'an old bookmarker given me by my mother. It is worked in silk, and, when I examine the wrong side of it, I see nothing but a tangle of threads crossed and recrossed. It looks like a big mistake. One would think that someone had done it who did not know what she was doing. But, when I turn it over and look at the right side, I see there, beautifully embroidered, the letters GOD IS LOVE. We are looking at all this to-day,' he concluded, 'from the wrong side. Some day we shall see it from another standpoint, and shall understand.' This all happened many years ago; but quite recently some who were present declared that they never forgot the story of the bookmarker and the comfort that it brought.

It was a bookmarker of exactly the same kind, and bearing precisely the same inscription, that brought the fragrance of roses into the dusty heart of Rodney Steele. Sitting alone in his Harley Street flat, he found himself turning over the pages of a Bible that belonged to Mrs. Jake, his housekeeper. Among those pages he found Mrs. Jake's marriage 'lines,' a photograph of her husband in military uniform, some pressed flowers and--a perforated bookmarker! And on the bookmarker, in pink silk, were embroidered the words: GOD IS LOVE. It reminded him of those far-off days in which, as a little boy, he had delighted in the possession of his first box of paints. He had begged his mother to give him something to color, and she had pricked out those very words on a card and asked him to paint them for her.

God! Love!

Love! God!
God is Love!

So said the bookmarker; but, he reflected sadly, *love* had failed him long ago, and of *God* he had no knowledge at all.

III

When those three tremendous words next confronted Rodney Steele, they were worked, not in silk, but in stone! In a lower flat, in the same building in Harley Street, there dwelt a Bishop's widow. Rodney got to know her, to like her, and, at last, to confide in her. One afternoon they were discussing the novel that all London was reading, *The Great Divide*. It was from his own pen, but he did not tell her so. Mrs. Bellamy--the widow--confessed that, in spite of its brilliance, she did not like it. It betrayed bitterness, a loss of ideals, a disbelief in love; it was not uplifting.

'It is life,' Rodney replied. 'Life tends to make a man lose faith in love.'

But Mrs. Bellamy would not hear of it.

'May I tell you,' she asked, 'the Bishop's way of meeting all difficulties, sorrows and perplexities?'

'Do tell me,' said Rodney.

'He met them with three little words, each of one syllable. Yet that sentence holds the truth of greatest import to our poor world; and its right understanding readjusts our entire outlook upon life, and should affect all our dealings with our fellow men: GOD IS LOVE. In our first home--a country parish in Surrey--three precious children were born to us--Griselda, Irene and little Launcelot. Scarlet fever and diphtheria broke out in the village, a terrible epidemic, causing grief and anxiety in many homes. We were almost worn out with helping our poor people-- nursing, consoling, encouraging. Then, just as the epidemic appeared to be abating, it reached our own home. Our darlings were stricken suddenly. Mr. Steele, we lost all three in a fortnight! My little Lancy was the last to go. When he died in my arms I felt I could bear no more.

'My husband led me out into the garden. It was a soft, sweet, summer night. He took me in his arms and stood long in silence, looking up to the quiet stars, while I sobbed upon his breast. At last he said, "My wife, there is one rope to which we must cling steadfastly, in order to keep our heads above water amid these overwhelming waves of sorrow. It has three golden strands. It will not fail us. GOD--IS--LOVE."

'The nursery was empty. There was no more patter of little feet; no children's merry voices shouted about the house. The three little graves in the churchyard bore the names Griselda, Irene and Launcelot; and on each we put the text, spelt out by the initials of our darlings' names: GOD IS LOVE. And in our own heart-life we experienced the great calm and peace of a faith which had come through the deepest depths of sorrow. We were sustained by the certainty of the love of God.'

Rodney Steele was deeply touched and impressed. Here was one who had known sorrow and had been sweetened by it. In her there was no trace of bitterness.

'I don't know,' he said to himself, as he came away, 'I don't know as to the truth of the Bishop's text; but, anyway, the Bishop's widow is love. She lives what she believes, and that certainly makes a belief worth having.'

'*God is love!*'--he had seen it worked in silk.

'*God is love*'--he had seen it inscribed three times in stone.

'*God is love!*'--he had seen it translated into actual life.

'*God is love!*'--he was almost persuaded to believe it.

IV

God is----!

It is the oldest question in the universe, and the greatest. It has been asked a million million times, and it would not have been altogether strange had we never discovered an answer. In Mr. H. G. Wells' story of the men who invaded the moon, he describes a conversation between the travelers and the Grand Lunar. The Grand Lunar asks them many questions about the earth which they are unable to answer. 'What?' he exclaims, 'knowing so little of **the earth**, do you attempt to explore **the moon**?' We men know little enough of **ourselves**: it would have been no cause for astonishment had we been unable to define **God**. Men lost themselves for ages in guess-work. They looked round about them; they saw how grandly a million worlds revolve, and they noticed how exquisitely the mighty forces of the earth are governed. Then they made their guess.

'***God is Power***,' they said, '***God is Power!***'

Then, peering a little more deeply into the heart of things, they saw that all these terrific forces are not only controlled, but harnessed to high ends. All things are working--they are working together--they are working together for good! And thereupon men made their second guess.

'***God is Wisdom***,' they said, '***God is Wisdom!***'

Then, observing things still more closely, men began to see great ethical principles underlying the laws of the universe. In the long run, evil suffers, and, in the long run, right is rewarded.

'***God is Justice***,' they said, '***God is Justice!***'

And so men made their guesses, and, as they guessed, they built. They erected temples, now to the God of Power, then to the God of Wisdom, and again to the God of Justice. They had yet to learn that they were worshiping the part and not the whole; they were worshiping the rays and not the Light Itself.

Then Jesus came, and men understood. By His words and His deeds, by His life and His death, He revealed the whole truth. God is Power and Wisdom and Justice--but He is more. In a European churchyard there stands a monument erected by a poet to his wife. It bears the inscription:

    She was----,   But words are wanting to say what!   Think what a wife should be   And she was that!

God is----! God is--what?

    He is----,   But words are wanting to say what!   Think what a God should be   And He is that!

Jesus filled in the age-long blank; He filled it in, not in cold language, but in warm life. Many attempts have been made to translate His definition from the terms of life into the terms of language. Only once have those attempts been even approximately successful. The words on the perforated bookmarker represent the best answer that human speech has ever given to the question.

God is----

God is--what?

GOD--IS--LOVE!

V

Rodney Steele met again the girl--ripened now into the full glory of womanhood--from whom he had been so cruelly separated. He felt that it was too late to right the earlier wrong; and, in any case, his life was too embittered to offer her now. But he rejoiced in her friendship, and, one day, opened his heart to her.

'Madge,' he said, 'I am furious with Fate. Life is chaos. Shall I tell you of what it reminds me? When I was last in Florence I was invited to the dress rehearsal of "Figli Di Re." I took my seat in the stalls of the huge empty opera house. The members of the orchestra were all in their places. Pandemonium reigned! Each man was playing little snatches of the score before him, all in the same key, but with no attempt at time, tune or order. The piping of the flute, the sighing of the fiddle, the grunt of the double bass, the clear call of the cornet, the bray of the trombones, all went on together. The confused hubbub of sound was indescribable. Suddenly a slim, alert figure leaped upon the estrade and struck the desk sharply with a baton. It was the maestro! There was instant silence. He looked to the right; looked to the left; raised his baton; and lo! full, rich, sweet, melodious, blending in perfect harmony, sounded the opening chords of the overture!'

Rodney likened the jangling discords to the confusion of his own life. There was in his soul a disappointed love, an implacable hate, and a medley of other discords.

'You are waiting for the Maestro, Roddie!' said Madge. 'His baton will reduce chaos to order with *a measure of three beats.*'

'Three beats?'

'Yes; three almighty beats: GOD--IS--LOVE!'

He shook his head.

'I left off pricking texts when I was five, and gave up painting when I was nine.'

'It is not what you do to the texts, Rodney; it is what the texts do to you!'

He left her, and, soon after, left London.

VI

Yes, he left her, and he left London; but he could not leave the text. It confronted him once more. He had taken refuge in a little fishing village on the East Coast. Up on the cliffs, among the corn-fields, flecked with their crimson poppies, he came upon a quaint old church. He stepped inside. In the porch was a painting of an old ruin--ivy-covered, useless and desolate--standing out, jagged and roofless, against a purple sky. The picture bore a striking inscription:

   The ruins of my soul repair   And make my heart a house of prayer.

'***The ruins of my soul!***' Rodney thought of the discord within.

'***Make my heart a house of prayer!***' Rodney thought of the maestro.

He passed out into the little graveyard on the very edge of the cliff. He was amused at the quaint epitaphs. Then one tombstone, lying flat upon the ground, a tombstone which, in large capitals, called upon the reader to 'Prepare to meet thy God,' startled him. Again he thought of the clashing discords of his soul.

'Then, suddenly,' says Mrs. Barclay, 'the inspired Word did that which It--and It alone--can do. It gripped Rodney and brought him face to face with realities--past, present and future--in his own inner life. At once, the Bishop's motto came into his mind; the three words his gentle mother used to draw that her little boy might paint them stood out clearly as the answer to all vague and restless questionings: GOD IS LOVE!'

'***God is Love!***'

'***Prepare to Meet thy God!***'

How could he, with his old hate in his heart, stand in the presence of a God of Love?

Standing there bareheaded, with one foot on the prone tombstone, Rodney grappled with the passion that he had cherished through the years, and thus took his first step along the path of preparation.

'I forgive the woman who came between us,' he said aloud. 'My God, I forgive her--as I hope to be forgiven!'

'As soon as a man comes to understand that **GOD IS LOVE**,' said Dr. Chalmers, 'he is infallibly converted.' That being so, Rodney Steele was infallibly converted that day, and that day he entered into peace.

VII

When Robert Louis Stevenson settled at Samoa, the islands were ablaze with tumult and strife. And, during those years of bitterness, Stevenson did his utmost to bring the painful struggle to an end. He visited the chiefs in prison, lavished his kindnesses upon the islanders, and made himself the friend of all. In the course of time the natives became devotedly attached to the frail and delicate foreigner who looked as though the first gust of wind would blow him away. His health required that he should live away on the hill-top, and they pitied him as he painfully toiled up the stony slope. To show their affection for him, they built a road right up to his house, in order to make the steep ascent more easy. And they called that road Ala Loto Alofa--***The Road to the Loving Heart***. They felt, as they toiled at their labor of gratitude, that they were not only conferring a boon on the white man, but that they were making a beaten path from their own doors to the heart that loved them all.

God is Love; and it is the glory of the everlasting Gospel that it points the road by which the Father's wayward sons--in whichever of the far countries they may have wandered--may find a way back to the Father's house, and home to the Loving Heart.

XI
THOMAS HUXLEY'S TEXT

I

She was a sermon-taster and was extremely sensitive to any kind of heresy. It is in his *Life of Donald John Martin*, a Presbyterian minister, that the Rev. Norman C. Macfarlane places her notable achievement on permanent record. He describes her as 'a stern lady who was provokingly evangelical.' There came to the pulpit one Sabbath a minister whose soundness she doubted. He gave out as his text the words: '***What doth the Lord require of thee but to do justly, to love mercy, and to walk humbly with thy God?*** ' '*Weel, weel,*' this excellent woman exclaimed, as she turned to her friend beside her, '*weel, weel, if there's one text in a' the Buik waur than anither, yon man is sure to tak' it!*'

II

She thought that text the ***worst*** in the Bible. Huxley thought it the ***best***. Huxley was, as everybody knows, the Prince of Agnostics. We need not stop to ask why. Nobody who has read the story of John Stuart Mill's boyhood will wonder that Mill was a skeptic. And nobody who has read the story of Thomas Huxley's boyhood will wonder at his becoming an agnostic. As Edward Clodd, his biographer, says, 'his boyhood was a cheerless time. Reversing Matthew Arnold's sunnier memories:

No rigorous teachers seized his youth,   And purged its faith and tried its fire,

Shewed him the high, white star of truth,   There bade him gaze, and there aspire.

'He told Charles Kingsley that he was "kicked into the world, a boy without guide or training, or with worse than none"; he "had two years of a pandemonium of a school, and, after that, neither help nor sympathy in any intellectual direction till he reached manhood."' And, even then, as those familiar with his biography know, he had little enough.

What would Huxley have been, I wonder, if the sympathy for which he hungered had been extended to him? If, instead of badgering him with arguments and entangling him in controversy, Mr. Gladstone and Bishop Wilberforce and others had honestly attempted to see things through his spectacles! Huxley was said to be as cold as ice and as inflexible as steel; but I doubt it. In his life-story I find two incidents--one belonging to his early manhood and one belonging to his age--which tell a very different tale.

The *first* is connected with the birth of his boy. It is the last night of the Old Year, and he is waiting to hear that he is a father. He spends the anxious hour in framing a resolution. In his diary he pledges himself 'to smite all humbugs, however big; to give a nobler tone to science; to set an example of abstinence from petty personal controversies and of toleration for everything but lying; to be indifferent as to whether the work is recognized as mine or not, so long as it is done. It is half-past ten at night. Waiting for my child. I seem to fancy it the pledge that all these things shall be.' And the next entry runs:

'*New Year's Day, 1859.* Born five minutes before twelve. Thank God!'

Mark that '*Thank God!*' and then note what follows. A year or two later, when the child is snatched from him, he makes this entry and then closes the journal for ever. He has no heart to keep a diary afterwards.

'Our Noel, our firstborn, after being for nearly four years our delight and our joy, was carried off by scarlet fever in forty-eight hours. This day week he and I had a great romp together. On Friday his restless head, with its bright blue eyes and tangled golden hair, tossed all day upon the pillow. On Saturday night I carried his cold, still body here into my study. Here, too, on Sunday night, came his mother and I to that holy leavetaking. My boy is gone; but in a higher and better sense than was in my mind when, four years ago, I wrote what stands above, I feel that my fancy has been fulfilled. I say heartily and without bitterness--Amen, so let it be!'

'*Thank God!*' exclaims our great Agnostic when the child is born.

'*Amen!*' he says, submissively, when the little one is buried.

This is the ***first*** of the two incidents. The ***second***--which is no less pathetic--is recorded by Dr. Douglas Adam. 'A friend of mine,' the doctor says, 'was acting on a Royal Commission of which Professor Huxley was a member, and one Sunday they were staying together in a little country town. "I suppose you are going to church," said Huxley. "Yes," replied my friend. "What if, instead, you stayed at home and talked to me of religion?" "No," was the reply, "for I am not clever enough to refute your arguments." "But what if you simply told me your own experience--what religion has done for you?" My friend did not go to church that morning; he stayed at home and told Huxley the story of all that Christ had been to him; and presently there were tears in the eyes of the great agnostic as he said, "***I would give my right hand if I could believe that!***"'

This, if you please, is the man who was supposed to be as cold as ice and as inflexible as steel! This is the man for whom the Christians of his time had nothing better than harsh judgments, freezing sarcasms and windy arguments! How little we know of each other! How slow we are to understand!

III

But the text! It was in the course of his famous--and furious--controversy with Mr. Gladstone that Huxley paid his homage to the text. He was pleading for a better understanding between Religion and Science.

'The antagonism between the two,' he said, 'appears to me to be purely fictitious. It is fabricated, on the one hand, by short-sighted religious people, and, on the other hand, by short-sighted scientific people.' And he declared that, whatever differences may arise between the ***exponents*** of Nature and the ***exponents*** of the Bible, there can never be any real antagonism between Science and Religion themselves. 'In the eighth century before Christ,' he goes on to say, 'in the eighth century before Christ, in the heart of a world of idolatrous polytheists, the Hebrew prophets put forth a conception of religion which appears to me to be as wonderful an inspiration of genius as the art of Pheidias or the science of Aristotle. "***What*** doth the Lord require of thee but to do justly and to love mercy and to walk humbly with thy God?*" If any so-called religion takes away from this great saying of Micah, I think it wantonly mutilates, while if it adds thereto, I think it obscures, the perfect ideal of religion.'

And it was on the ground of their common admiration for this text--the **worst** text in the world, the **best** text in the world--that Mr. Gladstone and Professor Huxley reached some kind of agreement. Not to be outdone by his antagonist, Mr. Gladstone raised his hat to the text.

'I will not dispute,' he says, 'that in these words is contained the true ideal of discipline and attainment. Still, I cannot help being struck with an impression that Mr. Huxley appears to cite these terms of Micah as if they reduced the work of religion from a difficult to an easy program. But look at them again. Examine them well. They are, in truth, in Cowper's words:

Higher than the heights above, Deeper than the depths beneath.

Do justly, that is to say, extinguish self; ***love mercy***, cut utterly away all the pride and wrath and all the cupidity that make this fair world a wilderness; ***walk humbly with thy God***, take his will and set it in the place where thine own was wont to rule. Pluck down the tyrant from his place; set up the true Master on His lawful throne.' In the text--the **worst** text in the Bible; the **best** text in the Bible--Mr. Gladstone and Professor Huxley find a trysting-place. We may therefore leave the argument at that point.

IV

The words with which Huxley fell in love were addressed by the prophet to a desperate man--and that man a king--who was prepared to pay any price and make any sacrifice if only, by so doing, he might win for himself the favor of the Most High. '***Wherewith shall I come before the Lord and bow myself before the high God?*** he cries. '***Shall I come before Him with burnt offerings, with calves a year old? Will the Lord be pleased with thousands of rams or with ten thousands of rivers of oil? Shall I give my firstborn for my transgression, the fruit of my body*** *for the sin of my soul?'*

'***My firstborn!***'--we have just witnessed a father's anguish on the death of his firstborn. But Balak, King of Moab, is prepared to lead his firstborn to the sacrificial altar if, by so doing, he can secure the favor of the Highest.

And the answer of the prophet is that the love of God is not for sale. And, if it ***were*** for sale, it could not be purchased by an act of immolation in which heaven could find no pleasure at all. F. D. Maurice points out, in one of his letters to R. H. Hutton, that the world has cherished two ideas of sacrifice. When a man discovers that his life is out of harmony with the divine Will, he may make a sacrifice by which he brings his conduct into line with the heavenly ideal. That is the one view. The other is Balak's. Balak hopes, by offering his child upon the altar, to bring the divine pleasure into line with his unaltered life. 'All light is in the one idea of sacrifice,' says Maurice, 'and all darkness in the other. The idea of sacrifice, not as an act of obedience to the divine will, but as a means of changing that will, is the germ of every dark superstition.'

Heaven is not to be bought, the prophet told the king. '**He hath shewed thee, O man, what is good; and what does the Lord require of thee but to do justly and to love mercy and to walk humbly with thy God?'**

Equity! Charity! Piety!
Do something! Love something! Be something!
Do justly! Love mercy! Walk humbly with thy God!

These, and these alone, are the offerings in which heaven finds delight.

V

I cannot help feeling sorry for the lady in the Scottish church. She thinks that Balaam's brave reply to Balak is the worst text in the Bible. And she is not alone. For, in his ***Literature and Dogma***, Matthew Arnold shows that she is the representative of a numerous and powerful class. 'In our railway stations are hung up,' Matthew Arnold says, 'sheets of Bible texts to catch the eye of the passer-by. And very profitable admonitions to him they generally are. One, particularly, we have all seen. It asks the prophet Micah's question: **Wherewith shall I come before the Lord and bow myself before the high God?** And it answers that question with one short quotation from the New Testament: **With the precious blood of Christ.**' Matthew Arnold maintains that this is not honest. By casting aside the prophet's answer, and substituting another, the people who arranged the placard ally themselves with the lady in the Scottish church. They evidently think Balaam's reply to Balak *the worst text in the Bible*. But is it? Is it good, is it fair, is it honest to strike out the real answer and to insert in its place an adopted one? I wish to ask the lady in the Scottish church--and the people who prepared the placard--two pertinent questions.

My *first* question is this. Is the deleted text--the worst text in the Bible--true? That is extremely important. **Does** God require that man should do justly, love mercy and walk humbly with Himself? Is it not a fact that heaven **does** insist on equity and charity and piety? Can there, indeed, be any true religion without these things? Do they not represent the irreducible minimum? If this be so, is it not as well for that Scottish minister to preach on that terrible text, after all? And, if this be so, would not the original answer to the question be the best answer for the placard?

My *second* question is this. Even from the standpoint of 'a stern lady who is provokingly evangelical,' is it not well for the minister to preach on that objectionable text? The lady is anxious, and commendably anxious, that the pulpit of her church should sound forth the magnificent verities of the Christian evangel. But will a man desire the salvation which the New Testament reveals unless he has first recognized his inability to meet heaven's just demands? In a notable fragment of autobiography, Paul declares that, but for the law, he would never have known the meaning of sin. It was when he heard how much he owed to the divine justice that he discovered the hopelessness of his bankruptcy. It was when he listened to the *Thou shalts* and the *Thou shalt nots* that he cried, 'O wretched man that I am: who shall deliver me?' It was Sinai that drove him to Calvary. The law, with its stern, imperative demands, was, he says, the schoolmaster that led him to Christ. The best way of showing that a stick is crooked is to lay a straight one beside it. This being so, the lady in the Scottish church, and the compilers of Matthew Arnold's placard, must consider whether, in the interests of that very evangelism for which they are so justly jealous, they can afford to supersede the stately passages that make men feel their desperate need of a Saviour.

This, at any rate, is the way in which Micah used the story of the conversation between Balak and Balaam. By means of it he sought to reduce the people to despair. And then, when they had fallen upon their faces and covered themselves with sackcloth, he made one of the noblest evangelical pronouncements that the Old Testament contains: '***He pardoneth iniquity because He delighteth in mercy: Thou wilt cast all their sins into the depths of the sea.***' But the people would never have listened hungrily to that glad golden word unless they had first realized the sublimity of the divine demand and the incalculable extent of their shortcoming.

VI

We each have a blind spot. We see truth fragmentarily. If only the excellent lady in the Scottish church could have seen, in the minister's text, what Huxley saw in it! But she didn't; and, because she was blind to its beauty, she called it '***the worst text in the Bible!***' And if only Huxley could have grasped those precious truths that were so dear to her! But he never did. He could only shake his fine head sadly and say, 'I do not know!' 'I would give my right hand,' he exclaims, 'if I could believe that!' Mr. Clodd adorns the title-page of his ***Life of Huxley*** with the words of Matthew Arnold: 'He saw life steadily and saw it whole.' That sad shake of the head, and that passionate but melancholy exclamation about giving his right hand, prove that the tribute is not quite true. Huxley, as he himself more than half suspected, missed the best.

When Sir George Adam Smith, in his ***Book of the Twelve Prophets***, comes to this great passage in Micah, he prints it in italics right across the page:

What doth the Lord require of thee but to do justly and to love mercy and to walk humbly with thy God?

This, says Sir George, is the greatest saying of the Old Testament; and there is only one other in the New which excels it:

Come unto Me, all ye that labor and are heavy laden, and I will give you rest.

Huxley had eyes for the *first*, but none for the *second*; the Scottish lady had eyes for the *second*, but none for the *first*; but they who 'see life steadily and see it whole' will stand up to salute the majesty of both.

VII

It is customary for the Presidents of the United States to select the passage which they shall kiss in taking the oath on assuming the responsibilities of their great office. President Harding had no hesitation in making his choice. He turned to this great saying of Micah. '***What doth the Lord require of thee but to do justly and to love mercy and to walk humbly with thy God?***' The lady in the Scottish church would frown and shake her head, but the President felt that, of all the texts in the Bible, ***that was the best***.

XII
WALTER PETHERICK'S TEXT

I

He was born at Islington on the day on which Sir Walter Raleigh was executed; and his father named him after the gallant knight whom he himself was so proud of having served. That was forty-seven years ago. He is now a prosperous London merchant, living, at ordinary times, over his warehouse, and delighting in the society of his four motherless children. At ordinary times! But these are not ordinary times. The plague is in the city! It appeared for the first time about two months ago and has gradually increased in virulence ever since. Mr. Petherick has therefore withdrawn with his two boys and his two girls to Twickenham. This morning--the morning of July 16, 1665--they all go together to the Parish Church. The riverside is in all its summer glory. The brilliant sunshine seems to mock both the wretchedness so near at hand and the heavy anxiety that weighs upon their hearts. During the week a solemn fast-day has been observed, and to-day, services of humiliation and intercession are to be held in all the churches. Several times, during the past week or two, Mr. Petherick has visited the city. It was a melancholy experience. Most of the shops were shut; poor creatures who claimed that they themselves or their relatives were infected by the pestilence cried for alms at every corner; and he had passed many houses on whose doors a red cross had been marked, and, underneath, the words, 'Lord, have mercy upon us!' To-day that pathetic entreaty is to be offered in every sanctuary. All through the country, men and women are pleading that the awful visitation may be stayed. At Twickenham the church soon fills, and the fervently murmured responses give evidence of the depth and intensity of the universal emotion. Mr. Petherick never forgot the sermon that was preached in the old church that July morning. At least, he never forgot the text. '***Although the fig tree shall not blossom, neither shall fruit be in the vines; the labor of the olive shall fail, and the fields shall yield no meat; the flocks shall be cut off from the fold, and there shall be no herd in the stalls; yet I will rejoice in the Lord and I will joy in the God of my salvation!***'

The fields barren! The stalls empty! The vineyards bare!
I will rejoice! I will joy! I will joy! I will rejoice!

The text reminded the Pethericks of the dazzling sunshine that, as they came along, had seemed so unsympathetic. For here was a radiance equally incongruous! Here was faith shining like a solitary star on a dark night! Here was joy, singing her song, like the nightingale, amidst the deepest gloom! It was as though a merry peal of bells was being rung on a day of public lamentation.

II

'The words took hold upon me mightily!' wrote Walter Petherick to a friend in 1682. I do not wonder. Quite apart from their singular application to his own case, they are full of nobility and grandeur. When, in 1782--exactly a century later--Benjamin Franklin was appointed American Plenipotentiary at Paris, some of the brilliant French wits of that period twitted him on his admiration for the Bible. He determined to test their knowledge of the Volume they professed to scorn. Entering their company one evening, he told them that he had been reading an ancient poem, and that its stately beauty had greatly impressed him. At their request he took from his pocket a manuscript and proceeded to read it. It was received with exclamations of extravagant admiration. 'Superb!' they cried. 'Who was the author? Where did Franklin discover it? How could copies be obtained?' He informed them, to their astonishment, that it was the third chapter of the prophecy of Habakkuk--the passage to which Mr. Petherick and his children listened that sad but sunny morning at Twickenham.

The Petherick incident belongs to the ***seventeenth*** century; the Franklin incident belongs to the ***eighteenth***; and they remind me of one that belongs to the ***nine-***

teenth. Daniel Webster was one morning discussing with a number of eminent artists the subjects commonly chosen for portrayal upon canvas. 'I have often wondered,' he said, 'that no painter has yet thought it worth his while to draw his inspiration from one of the most sublime passages in any literature.' 'And what is that?' they asked. 'Well,' he replied, 'what finer conception for a masterpiece could any artist desire than the picture of the prophet Habakkuk sitting in the midst of utter ruin and desolation, singing, in spite of everything, faith's joyous and triumphant song?'

III

Suppose!
It is a ***Song of Suppositions***!
'***Suppose*** the fig tree shall not blossom!'
'***Suppose*** the vine shall bear no fruit!'
'***Suppose*** the labor of the olive shall fail!'
'***Suppose*** the fields shall yield no corn!'
'***Suppose*** the flock shall be cut off from the fold!'
'***Suppose*** there shall be no herd in the stalls!'
'***Suppose! Suppose! Suppose!***'

I very well remember a conversation I once had at Mosgiel with old Jeanie McNab. Jeanie subsisted on a mixed diet of smiles and songs.

'But, supposing, Jeanie----' I began one day.

'Now don't you have anything to do with ***supposings***,' she exclaimed. 'I know them all. "***Suppose*** I should lose my money!" "***Suppose*** I should lose my health!" And all the rest. When those ***supposings*** come knocking at your heart, you just slam the door, and bolt it, and don't let any of them in!'

It was excellent advice; yet the prophet acted on a diametrically opposite principle. When the ***supposings*** came knocking at his door, he cried 'Come in!' and in they came!

'***Suppose*** the figs are barren!'

'*Suppose* the vines wither!'
'*Suppose* the olive fail!'
'*Suppose* the corn perish!'
'*Suppose* the sheep starve!'
'*Suppose* the cattle die!'

The prophet invites them all to come in. They jostle each other as they throng his little room. He hears all that they have to say, and then he answers them.

'Whence came all these things?' he demands. 'Whence came the figs and the vines and the olives, the corn and the flocks and the herds?' And, having asked this question, he himself proceeds to answer it.

'*HE* gave them!' he cries triumphantly, '*HE* gave them! And if they perish, as you *suppose*, *He* can as easily replace them! *Therefore will I rejoice in the Lord and will joy in the God of my salvation!* It is a small thing to lose the *gifts* as long as you possess the *Giver*; the supreme tragedy lies in losing the *Giver* and retaining only the *gifts*!'

There is no record as to what the preacher said that Sunday morning at Twickenham; but some such thoughts as these must have been suggested to the eager minds of the Pethericks as they listened so attentively. 'The words took hold upon me mightily!' the father confessed, in a letter to a friend, long afterwards.

IV

That evening a horror of great darkness fell upon the soul of Walter Petherick. He spent the sunset hours quietly with the young people, and, before they bade each other good-night, he read with them again the passage that had so impressed them in the morning. Then, left to himself, Mr. Petherick put on his hat and took a stroll in the lane. It was a perfect summer's evening, warm and star-lit; yet its peace failed to penetrate his tortured soul. A glow-worm twinkled in the grass under the hedge, but no ray of light pierced the impenetrable gloom within. He returned to his room, and, after sitting for a while at the open window, looking down on the sluggish waters of the tranquil river, he threw himself on his knees beside his bed. One by one he prayed for each of his children. The red cross that he had seen on so many doors seemed to have stamped itself upon the retina of his eye; it blazed before him even whilst the lids were closed in prayer.

'Lord, have mercy on us!' said the legend under the cross.

'Lord, have mercy on us!' cried Mr. Petherick over and over and over again.

He thought of the morning's text, but it only mocked him, as the sunshine mocked him on his way to church.

'I could not say it,' he moaned. 'If my children were snatched from me--my fine boys and my lovely girls--the treasures that *she* left me--how could I ***rejoice in the Lord and joy in the God of my salvation?***'

He broke into a fresh outburst of supplication. Again he mentioned each of his children by name. 'Spare him; oh, spare him!' he cried; and, as he thought of the girls, 'Spare her, O Lord; have pity, I beseech Thee!'

He wiped his face; it was damp with perspiration. He allowed his forehead to rest upon his folded arms; and then, bowed there in the solitude of his room and in the stillness of the summer night, a strange thought took possession of him.

V

He remembered to have prayed as fervently as this before--many, many years ago. In those days--the days of his earliest religious experiences--he had prayed, almost as earnestly as this, for his own spiritual prosperity, for the extension of Christ's Kingdom and for the enlightenment of the world. It seemed like a dream as he recalled it. He was scarcely more than a boy in those days. The ardor and intensity of that distant time had deserted him so gradually, and had vanished so imperceptibly, that he had never missed it until now. Love had come into his life, irradiating and transfiguring everything. Love had led to marriage; four happy children had brought added gladness to his home and fresh contentment to his heart; and he had abandoned himself without reserve to these domestic cares and comforts. The things that had so completely captivated his soul were all of them *good* things--just as the fig and the vine and the olive, the corn and the flocks and the herds were all of them *good* things--but he had allowed them to elbow out the wealthiest things of all. The *good* had become the enemy of the *best*. Before his heart had been gladdened by those treasures that were now so dear to him, he had every day *rejoiced in the Lord and joyed in the God of his salvation*. But not since! His enrichment had proved his impoverishment! What was it that the preacher had said? 'It is a small thing to love the ***gifts*** as long as you possess the ***Giver***; the supreme tragedy lies in losing the ***Giver*** and retaining only the ***gifts***.' And Walter Petherick felt that night that that supreme tragedy was his.

He rose from his knees, reached for his Bible, and turned once more to the chapter from which the minister had preached. '*O Lord*,' it began, '*revive Thy work in the midst of years!*' He himself was '*in the midst of years.*' The thought brought with it a sense of shame and a rush of thankfulness. He was ***ashamed*** that he had permitted the years that had gone to filch so much from him. Like waves that strew treasures on the shore, and snatch treasures from the shore, he felt that the years had brought much and taken much. Yet he felt grateful that he was still '*in the midst of the years*'; it is better to discover life's loss at the halfway house than to find it out at the end of the journey! He returned the Bible to its place, and, as he did so, he closed his eyes and repeated for himself the prophet's prayer.

'*O Lord*,' he cried, '*revive Thy work in the midst of the years; in the midst of the years make known; in wrath remember mercy!*'

It seemed as if the prayer had opened the gates of his soul to the peace of the night. As he looked again at the glistening river, he felt strangely soothed and comforted. And, half an hour later, he was sleeping as restfully as any of his children.

VI

Once more it is a Sunday evening, and once more we are at Twickenham. For at Twickenham the family have now made their home; they never, after the Plague Year, resided in the city. More than twelve months have passed. We last saw them on July 16, 1665; this is Sunday, September 2, 1666. And this Sunday has been as eventful and as memorable as that. For, just as the family were assembling at the breakfast table, Henry, the elder of the two boys, burst into the room, exclaiming excitedly:

'Father, the city is on fire!'

It was true! London was one great sea of flame! In the afternoon the father and the two sons drove as far as the Borough; it was as near as they could get to the raging conflagration. And what a sight confronted them! Immense tongues of crimson shot up from the burning city and seemed to lick the very skies. When the clouds of smoke parted for a moment, they saw towers falling, walls collapsing, chimneys tottering, whilst the crash of roof after roof kept up a series of reports that resembled the firing of artillery. Every now and again a terrific explosion rent the air, followed immediately by an eruption of flaming debris that looked volcanic in its weird grandeur. London seemed to be in the grip of an angry demon that was bent on tearing it to fragments. The fire exhibited a thousand fantastic forms; it blazed in every conceivable hue and color; it roared and shrieked and sputtered; it hissed and thundered and growled. A spectacle of such vivid beauty, yet of such awful horror, had never been seen in England before. And, somewhere within the area swept by that red, red ocean of flame, was Mr. Petherick's warehouse containing all, or practically all, his earthly possessions!

But that Sunday night the soul of Walter Petherick knew no such anguish as it had known a year ago. He thought of the '***supposes***.' He read once more the prophet's song of defiance and of triumph. He smiled to himself as he reflected that the flames could only take the ***gifts***; they could not rob him of the ***Giver***. '*Therefore*,' he said to himself, '***I will rejoice in the Lord and joy in the God of my salvation***'; for 'it is a small thing to lose the ***gifts*** as long as you possess the ***Giver***; the supreme tragedy lies in losing the ***Giver*** and retaining only the ***gifts***!' And that Sunday night, whilst London crackled and blazed, the sleep of Walter Petherick was once more like the sleep of a little child.

VII

Again it is a Sunday evening at Twickenham. Walter Petherick has been celebrating his fiftieth birthday. Three years have passed since the Great Plague and two since the Great Fire. In the presence of the young people, he has poured out his heart in reverent gratitude for the mercies that have so richly crowned his days. And now, the soft autumn day, with its russet tints and its misty sunlight having closed, he is once more alone in his room.

'O Lord,' he prays, 'Thou hast been pleased by pestilence and by fire to redeem my soul from destruction. Thou didst threaten me with the loss of Thy choicest ***gifts*** that I might set my heart's affections once more upon their ***Giver***. But the fig tree did not wither; the vines did not perish; the olive did not fail. The pestilence did not touch my children; the flames did not destroy my goods. Accept the thanks of Thy servant this day and help him, all his days, ***to rejoice in the Lord and to joy in the God of his salvation***.'

And the records show that Walter Petherick lived to enjoy long life, abounding wealth, great honors, and the clinging affection of his children's children. And ever in his heart he cherished a deep, deep secret and sang a rapturous song. For he reveled, not only in the ***gifts***, but in the ***Giver***. He rejoiced in ***the Lord*** and joyed in ***the God of his salvation***.

XIII
DOCTOR BLUND'S TEXT

I

The doctor was the worst man in Bartown, and that was saying a good deal. For Bartown had the reputation of being 'the wickedest little hole in all England.' It is Harold Begbie who, in *The Vigil*, tells its story. Dr. Blund, he assures us, spent most of his time drinking gin and playing billiards at 'The Angel.' In a professional point of view, only one person in the little seaside town believed in him, and that was the broken and bedraggled little woman whose whole life had been darkened by his debauchery. Mrs. Blund was never tired of singing the doctor's praises. When she introduced him to a newcomer, and told of his wondrous cures and amazing skill, he listened like a man in a dream. 'Dr. Blund,'--so runs the story--'Dr. Blund was twitching with excess of alcohol, and only muttered and frowned as his wife talked of his powers. The terrible old doctor, with his hairy, purple face and his sunken eyes, seemed to think that his wife was doing him the most dreadful dis-service. It was wonderful that this little woman, instead of shrinking from exhibiting her husband, should have so pathetic a faith in the dreadful-looking rogue that she evidently fancied that he had but to be seen to be chosen as medical adviser.'

Thus the story opens. It could scarcely be expected that such a wreck could hold together for long. Exactly half-way through the book I find Mr. Rodwell, the young rector, standing at the street-corner talking to Mr. Shorder, the wealthy manufacturer. They are interrupted. Mrs. Blund comes hurrying breathlessly round the corner.

'Mr. Rodwell,' she pants, 'please come at once! Dr. Blund! He's asking for you! I've been to the vicarage, I've been everywhere, hunting for you. Don't delay a moment, please!'

Richard Rodwell was an earnest young clergyman, who had ideas of his own about things; and the task to which he was now summoned was very little to his taste. He saw in Blund a man who had lived hideously and was now concerned to avert his just punishment. He tried to believe that there was some hope for such a wretch; but the attempt was not altogether successful. He bent over the dying man and talked of mercy and repentance and forgiveness. But the words did not come from his own soul, and they did not comfort the soul of the man to whom they were addressed.

'There's something else!' he gasped.

'There is nothing outside the mercy of God,' replied the vicar.

'It's in the Bible, what I mean,' returned the dying man.

'What is it?' asked Rodwell soothingly.

'It's a text, "Except a man be **born again**----" You know the words, **Born again**. What does that mean?'

The doctor, in his professional capacity, had often seen a child draw its first breath, and had been impressed by its utter pastlessness. It had nothing to regret, nothing to forget. Everything was before it; nothing behind. And here was a text that seemed to promise such an experience a second time! To be **born again**! What was it to be **born again**? The dying doctor asked his insistent question repeatedly, but the vicar was out of his depth. He floundered pitifully. At last the doctor, to whom every moment was precious beyond all price, lost patience with the hesitating minister and changed the form of his question. Looking fixedly into his visitor's eyes, he exclaimed:

'Tell me, have *you* been **born again**?' Rodwell hung his head in silence, and the voice from the bed went on.

'Have you ever known in your life,' he asked, 'a moment when you felt that a great change happened to you? Are you pretending? Have you ever been conscious of *a new birth* in your soul?'

The vicar fenced with the question, but it was of no avail. The dying man raised himself suddenly on an elbow. 'You can't help me!' he cried angrily. He seized

Rodwell's wrist and held it tightly, fiercely. As he spoke, the fingers tightened their grasp, and he bent Rodwell's hand down to the bed, as it were for emphasis.

'You don't know,' he cried. 'You're pretending. The words you say are words for the living. I am a dying man. Have you the same message for the living and the dying? Have I a lifetime before me in which to work out repentance? You can't help me! You don't know! You have never been **born again**!'

Such a rebuke smites a minister like the sudden coming of the Day of Judgment. After his conversion John Wesley wrote a terrible letter to his old counselor, William Law. 'How will you answer to our common Lord,' he asks, 'that you, sir, never led me into light? Why did I scarcely ever hear you name the **name of Christ**? Why did you never urge me to **faith in His blood**? I beseech you, sir, to consider whether the true reason of your never pressing this salvation upon me was not this--***that you never had it yourself***!'

'It was a terrible discovery to make,' says Mr. Begbie. 'To think that he--Richard Rodwell, Vicar of Bartown--knew so little of the nature of God that he could say no single word that had significance for this dying soul! He was dumb. The words on his lips were the words of the Church. Out of his own heart, out of his own soul, out of his own experience, he could say nothing.'

'Forgive me,' he said, as he bent over the form on the bed, 'forgive me for failing you. It is not Christ who has failed; it is I.' He turned to go. The dying man opened his eyes and looked at Rodwell sadly and tragically.

'Try to learn what those words mean,' he muttered. '***Born again!*** It's the bad man's only chance.'

They parted, never to meet again; and from another minister's lips the doctor learned the secret for which he craved.

II

It is very difficult to excuse Mr. Rodwell, especially when we remember that the words that the dying doctor found so captivating, and that he himself found so perplexing, were originally intended to meet just such cases as that of Dr. Blund.

'What is it to be ***born again***? How can a man be ***born again***?' asked the voice from the bed.

'How can a man *be born* when he is old?' asked Nicodemus, as he heard the Saviour's words uttered for the first time.

'When he is old!' To Nicodemus, as to Dr. Blund, there was something singularly attractive about the thought of babyhood, the thought of pastlessness, the thought of beginning life all over again. But to the aged ruler, as to the aged doctor, it was an insoluble enigma, an inscrutable mystery.

'*How?*' asked Nicodemus of the Saviour. '*How* can a man *be born* when he is old?'

'*How?*' asked Dr. Blund of Mr. Rodwell. '*How* can a man be *born again?*'

We all feel that, unless the gospel can meet just such cases as these, we might almost as well have no gospel at all. And yet we have also felt the force of that persistent and penetrating *How?*

Dr. Blund is no frolic of Mr. Begbie's imagination. Dr. Blund is the representative of all those--and their name is legion--who, in the crisis of the soul's secret history, have turned towards the Saviour's strange saying with the most intense wistfulness and yearning. Let me cite three instances--each as unlike the others as it could possibly be--in order to show that all sorts and conditions of men have at some time felt as Dr. Blund felt in those last hours of his. John Bunyan, the tinker of Bedford, was born in the *seventeenth* century; the Duke of Wellington, soldier and statesman, was born in the *eighteenth* century; Frederick Charrington, the London brewer, was born in the *nineteenth* century. From a great cloud of available witnesses I select these three.

As to John Bunyan, the story of the beginnings of grace in the dreamer's soul is familiar to us all, but it will do us no harm to hear it from his own lips once again. 'Upon a day,' he says, 'the good providence of God called me to Bedford, to work at my calling; and in one of the streets of that town I came to where there were three or four poor women sitting in the sun talking about the things of God; and being now willing to hear them discourse, I drew near to hear what they said; but I heard, yet understood not; they were far above, out of my reach; for their talk was about *a new birth*!'

'*Their talk was about a new birth!*'

'Ye must be born again!'
'I heard,' says Bunyan, *'but I understood not!'*

'At this,' he goes on to say, 'at this I felt my heart begin to shake, for I saw that in all my thoughts about salvation, ***the new birth*** did never enter into my mind!'

Thus the soul of the sleeper awoke. He walked the streets of Bedford asking the old, old question, the question of Nicodemus, the question of Dr. Blund, the question of us all. 'How can a man be ***born again***? How can a man be ***born again***?'

From John Bunyan to the Duke of Wellington seems a far cry. But the transition may not be as drastic as it appears. Dr. W. H. Fitchett, who has made a special study of the character and achievements of the great Duke, recently told the story of a remarkable and voluminous correspondence that took place between Wellington and a young lady named Miss Jenkins. To this earnest and devout girl, her faith was the biggest thing in life. She had but one passionate and quenchless desire: the desire to share it with others. She sought for converts everywhere. A murderer awaited execution in the local gaol. Miss Jenkins obtained permission to visit him. She entered the condemned cell, pleaded with him, wept over him, won him to repentance, and the man went to the scaffold blessing her.

Then, from the winning of the lowest, she turned to the winning of the highest. She fastened her eyes upon the Duke of Wellington, the victor of Waterloo, the statesman of the hour, the most commanding figure in the three kingdoms. Wellington was then sixty-five, a man covered with honor and absorbed in public affairs. But, to Miss Jenkins, he was simply a great worldly figure, and, in 1834, she wrote a letter--a letter winged by many prayers--warning him of the peril of living without a sure, deep consciousness of the forgiveness of sins, through the redemption of Jesus Christ. Wellington's iron nature was strongly moved. He replied by return of post, and thus inaugurated a correspondence in the course of which he wrote to Miss Jenkins no fewer than three hundred and ninety letters. In the course of this amazing correspondence, Miss Jenkins begged for an interview, and it was granted. Miss Jenkins took out her New Testament and read to the old warrior these very words. '***Verily, verily, I say unto thee, except a man be born again, he cannot see the Kingdom of God!***' 'Here,' says Dr. Fitchett, in unfolding the story, 'here was a preacher of quite a new type! A girl's lips were reciting Christ's tremendous words: "***Ye must be born again!***" She was addressing them directly to him, and her uplifted finger was challenging him. Some long-dormant religious sensibilities awoke within him. The grace of the speaker, and the mystic quality of the thing spoken, arrested him.' To the end of his days the Duke firmly believed that, by means of this girl-prophet, God Himself spoke to his soul that day.

Mr. Frederick Charrington's story has been put on record by Guy Thorne. He was the son of the great brewer, the heir to more than a million pounds, and his time was very largely his own. He traveled and formed friendships. One of his earliest friends was Lord Garvagh. They traveled together, and, when they parted, Lord Garvagh asked Charrington if he would grant him one request. 'When you are quite alone,' his lordship pleaded, 'I should like you to read slowly and carefully the third chapter of John's Gospel!' Later on, Charrington met William Rainsford, and the acquaintance ripened into intimacy. 'Do you know what I wish you would do, Fred?' Rainsford said to him one day. 'I wish, when you are by yourself, that you would study the third chapter of the Gospel of John!'

'This is a very curious thing,' Charrington said to himself. 'My old friend, Lord Garvagh, and my new friend, Rainsford, both say exactly the same thing; and they both profess to be saved.'

Thus doubly challenged, he read the chapter with the closest attention, and was arrested by the words: '***Verily, verily, I say unto thee, Except a man be born again, he cannot see the Kingdom of God!***' 'As I read,' he says, 'light came into my soul,' and he ever afterwards regarded that moment as the turning-point of his whole life.

III

Now, what did these men--these and a hundred thousand more--see in the strange, mysterious words that Jesus spoke to the aged ruler twenty centuries ago? That is the question, and the question is not a difficult one to answer.

A new birth! To be ***born again***! What can it mean? It can only mean one thing. 'I wish,' somebody has sung----

I wish that there were some wonderful place   Called the Land of Beginning Again,   Where all our mistakes and all our heartaches   And all of our poor, selfish grief   Could be dropped, like a shabby old coat, at the door,   And never put on any more.

The words, if they mean anything, mean that there *is* such a place. A man *may* have a fresh start. In describing the greatest change that took place in his life--the greatest change that can take place in any man's life--Frank Bullen says: 'I love that description of conversion as the "**new birth**." No other definition touches the truth of the process at all. So helpless, so utterly knowledgeless, possessing nothing but the vague consciousness of life just begun!' Dr. Blund was thinking of the babes whose first breath he had seen drawn. So innocent; so pastless! Oh, to begin where they were beginning! Oh, to be ***born again***!'

Dr. Blund cannot begin where they were beginning. He cannot enjoy again--at any rate in this world--the opportunities of growth and development that were theirs. But he can be ***born again***! He can start afresh! Dr. Blund made that discovery on his deathbed, and, in talking of the dead doctor's experience, the young minister made the same discovery a day or two later. He felt his need; he turned in an agony of supplication to the Saviour whom he had so often preached; and he, too, entered into the new life.

'He made the great discovery,' Harold Begbie says. 'It had happened; the longed-for event had come; he stood by himself, all by himself, conscious now of the heart; no longer satisfied either with his own intellect or the traditions of a church. The miracle had happened. He had discovered the helplessness of humanity. He had discovered the need of the soul. He had begun at last to see into the heart of things.' He had been ***born again***!

There are two kinds of progress. There is the progress that moves away from infancy towards youth, towards maturity, towards age and decrepitude. And there is a higher progress, a progress that moves towards infancy. 'Except ye be converted and become as little children,' Jesus said, 'ye shall not enter into the kingdom of God.' And the only way of becoming a little child once more is by being ***born again***. It is the glory of the gospel that it offers a man that chance.

XIV
HEDLEY VICARS' TEXT

I

'*Those words are the sheet-anchor of my soul!*' said Hedley Vicars, a gallant young Army officer, as he sat talking to his sweetheart in the handsome drawing-room at Terling Place.

'*Those words are more golden than gold!*' exclaimed Miss Frances Ridley Havergal, and she ordered that they should be inscribed upon her tomb.

'*Those words did give a great ease to my spirit!*' John Bunyan tells us.

'*Those words*,' said old Donald Menzies, the mystic of Drumtochty, '*those words fell upon me like a gleam from the Mercy-seat!*'

What words? Let us return to Hedley Vicars! He was only twenty-eight when he fell, leading his regiment--the Ninety-seventh--in action before Sebastopol. The enemy attacked suddenly under cover of the darkness. 'The men of the Ninety-seventh behaved with the utmost gallantry and coolness,' said Lord Raglan, in the historic dispatch that reached England on Good Friday, 1855. 'They were led by Captain Vicars, who, unfortunately, lost his life in the engagement; and I am assured that nothing could be more distinguished than the gallantry and good example which he set to the detachment under his command.' His biographer tells us that it was more than three years earlier--in November, 1851--that, whilst awaiting in his room the return of a brother officer, he idly turned over the leaves of a Bible which lay on the table. The words, '*The blood of Jesus Christ, His Son, cleanseth us from all sin*,' caught his eyes and profoundly impressed his mind. 'If,' he said, as he closed the sacred Volume, 'if this be true, I will henceforth live by the grace of God as a man should live who has been redeemed by the blood of Jesus Christ.' That night he could scarcely sleep; the great words repeated themselves again and again within his throbbing brain; they seemed too good to be true.

'All sin! All sin!'

'Cleanseth from all sin!'

'The blood of Jesus Christ, His Son, cleanseth us from all sin.'

He never tired of telling of that wonderful experience. Miss Marsh, to whom he was engaged to be married, says that, almost as soon as they were first introduced to each other, 'he gave her an outline of the manner in which God had worked the great change in his heart. With forceful simplicity he told the point of the story; how the words, "*The blood of Jesus Christ, His Son, cleanseth us from all sin*," became the sheet-anchor of his soul, adding, "Thus was I born again of the Word of God which liveth and abideth for ever!"'

II

Away back in the infancy of the world I hear one of the earliest of the Patriarchs uttering a great and bitter cry. '*I have sinned!*' he cries; '*what shall I do?*' And, as I turn over the leaves of my Bible, I find that question echoed again and again, generation after generation and age after age. Yet never once does it receive the slightest hint or suggestion of an answer. And, depend upon it, if the Son of Man had never come into the world, it would have echoed round the globe--still unanswered and unanswerable--until this day. 'O Plato, Plato!' cried Socrates, 'it may be that the gods can forgive sin, but, alas, I do not see how!' Nor anybody else. Job's question fell back upon his face; the universe could give him no reply. It is very striking. And so, here at the beginning of my Bible, I hear the first man's question; and, here at the end of my Bible, I hear the last man's answer!

'What shall I do? What shall I do?'

'I have sinned; what shall I do?'

'The blood of Jesus Christ, His Son, cleanseth us from all sin!'

III

These two men--Job and John--present us, first with a *comparison*, and then with a *contrast*. It is interesting to examine side by side their views of the sin that represented so terrific a problem.

Job thought of it as a ***contaminating*** thing. He felt that his soul was soiled. 'What shall I do?' he cries, 'what shall I do? If I bathe myself in snow water and wash my hands never so clean, yet shalt Thou plunge me in the ditch and mine own clothes shall abhor me!' Every day of his life he thought he heard, morning and noon and night, the awful Voice of the Most High. 'Though thou wash thee with niter, and take thee much soap, yet thine iniquity is marked before Me, saith the Lord God.' He felt as Macbeth felt when advised to cleanse the stain from his guilty hands.

Will all great Neptune's ocean wash this blood Clean from my hand! No, this my hand will rather The multitudinous seas incarnadine, Making the green one red!

Job was like the old lama, in Rudyard Kipling's ***Kim***, who, year after year, wandered through cities and rice-fields, over the hills and across the plains, always searching, but searching in vain, for the River, the River of the Arrow, the River that could cleanse from sin!

John, on the other hand, thought of sin as a ***condemning*** thing. The great word 'condemnation' occurs on almost every page of his writings. He feels that every man's sin carries its own conviction. It is like finger-print evidence; it speaks for itself; it needs no long procession of corroborating witnesses. There it is! It tells its own terrible tale, and there is no gainsaying it.

IV

And yet, looked at in another way, the thoughts of these two men stand in sharp and striking contrast, the one with the other. '***I have sinned***,' cried Job; '***what*** shall I do? What shall I do?'

But there is no reply. In the course of the stupendous drama that bears his name, Job scours sea and land, earth and sky, for some answer to the wild questionings of his soul. He climbs the summits of the loftiest mountains and thrids the labyrinth of the deepest mine; he calls to the heights of the heavens and to the depths of the sea. But there is no answering voice, and he is left to nurse his dumb and piteous despair. Every attempt that he makes to rid his soul of its defilement is like the effort of a man who, in trying to remove the stain from his window, rubs on the wrong side of the glass.

But, in contrast with all this, John saw the Cross! How could he ever forget it? Had he not stood beside it, gazed into the thorn-crowned face, and received from those quivering lips their last sacred bequest--the charge of the Saviour's mother? And, all through the eventful years that followed, John never tired of presenting the Cross as the only answer to the Patriarch's question. He may not have perfectly understood it--no man ever yet comprehended all its heights and sounded all its depths! But it is easier to accept it than to reject it. For, if I reject it, I am confronted by an enigma even more unanswerable than Job's.

Oh, why was He there as the Bearer of sin   If on Jesus my guilt was not laid?
Oh, why from His side flowed the sin-cleansing stream,   If His dying my debt has not paid?

If, that is to say, the Cross is not the divine answer to the mystery of all the ages, then who shall attempt to solve the dark, inscrutable, impenetrable mystery of the Cross?

V

But it is! Experience proves it! In the course of his dazzling Apocalypse, John tells us that he saw a war being waged in heaven; and the hosts of righteousness overcame their powerful and sinister foes by the virtue of the blood of the Lamb. I do not know what he means--never expect to know in this world. But I know that, in this life, something very like it happens every day.

Martin Luther says that, in one of his periods of depression at the Wartburg, it seemed to him that he saw a hideous and malignant form inscribing the record of his own transgressions round the walls of his room. There seemed to be no end to the list--sins of thought, sins of word, sins of deed, sins of omission, sins of commission, secret sins, open sins--the pitiless scribe wrote on and on interminably. Whilst the accuser was thus occupied, Luther bowed his head and prayed. When he looked up again, the writer had paused, and, turning, faced him.

'Thou hast forgotten just one thing!' said Luther.

'And that--?' asked his tormentor.

'Take thy pen once more and write across it all: "***The blood of Jesus Christ, His Son, cleanseth us from all sin!***"' And, at the utterance of those words, the spirit vanished and the walls were clean!

In his ***Grace Abounding***, Bunyan tells us of a period in his life during which his soul seemed to be held in fetters of brass; and, every step he took, he took to the sound of the clanking of chains. 'But about ten or eleven o'clock on a certain day,' he says, 'as I was walking under a hedge (full of sorrow and guilt, God knows), suddenly this sentence rushed in upon me, "***The blood of Jesus Christ, His Son, cleanseth us from all sin.***" At this I made a stand in my spirit and began to conceive peace in my soul, and methought I saw as if the tempter did leer and steal away from me, as being ashamed of what he had done. At the same time also I had my sin and the blood of Christ thus represented to me: that my sin, when compared to the blood of Christ, was no more to it than this little clod or stone is to the vast and wide field that here I see. This gave me good encouragement.'

Neither Martin Luther nor John Bunyan would object to my setting them in the company of Donald Menzies. For, like them, Donald was at war with principalities and powers, with the rulers of the darkness of this world, with spiritual wickedness in high places. In the lonely anguish of that grim struggle it seemed as though, at the last, the gates of hell must have prevailed against him.

'Then,' he says, 'I heard a voice, oh, yes, as plain as you are hearing me: "***The blood of Jesus Christ, His Son, cleanseth us from all sin.***" It was like a gleam from the Mercy-seat, but I waited to see whether Satan had any answer and my heart was standing still. But there was no word from him, not one word. Then I leaped to my feet and cried, "Get thee behind me, Satan!" And I looked round, and there was no one to be seen but Janet in her chair with the tears on her cheeks, and she was saying, "Thanks be to God which giveth us the victory through our Lord Jesus Christ!"'

'*When I uttered those words,*' says Luther, '*the evil spirit vanished and the walls were clean!*'

'*When I made a stand upon those words,*' says Bunyan, '*the tempter did steal away from me and I entered into peace!*'

'*When I heard those words,*' says Donald Menzies, '*I waited to see if Satan had any answer, but there was no word from him, not one word!*'

This, surely, is what the seer means when he says that he saw all the hosts of evil routed and scattered by the virtue of the blood of the Lamb.

VI

Down at the library yesterday afternoon I spent an hour in glancing through the various volumes of Southey's **Commonplace Book**. And, among a vast assortment of musty notes that are now of interest to nobody, I came upon this: 'I have been reading of a man on the Malabar coast who had inquired of many devotees and priests as to how he might make atonement for his sins. At last he was directed to drive iron spikes, sufficiently blunted, through his sandals, and on these spikes he was to place his naked feet and then walk a distance of five hundred miles. He undertook the journey, but loss of blood and exhaustion of body compelled him to rest one day under the shade of a spreading tree. As he lay there, a missionary approached and began to preach the gospel. He announced as his theme the words: "*The blood of Jesus Christ, His Son, cleanseth us from all sin.*" Whilst the evangelist still preached, the man sprang up, tore off his sandals, and cried aloud: "That is what I want! That is what I want!" And he became a living witness to the fact that the redeeming blood of Christ **does** cleanse from human guilt.'

'*That is what I want!*' cried Southey's pilgrim on the coast of Malabar.

'*That is what I want!*' cried Luther in the Wartburg.

'*That is what I want!*' cried Bunyan at Bedford.

'*That is what I want!*' cried Donald Menzies at Drumtochty.

A Handful of Stars - Texts That Have Moved Great Minds 115

'*That is what I want!*' exclaimed young Hedley Vicars, as his startled eyes fell upon the tremendous words that seemed to leap from the Bible on the table. '***The blood of Jesus Christ, His Son, cleanseth us from all sin.***' 'That is what I want! That is what I want!'

Hedley Vicars appropriated the priceless gift held out to him, and his whole life was transfigured in consequence. His life--and his death! For, on that fatal night before Sebastopol, it was with Hedley Vicars as it was with the soldier with whom the poet has familiarized us. Everybody knows the story. Two men of God moved in the darkness across the field on which, that day, a battle had been fought.

And now they stand   Beside a manly form, outstretched alone.   His helmet from his head had fallen. His hand   Still firmly grasped his keen but broken sword.   His face was white and cold, and, thinking he was gone,   They were just passing on, for time was precious,   When a faint sigh caught their attentive ears. Life was still there, so bending down,   They whispered in his ears most earnestly, Yet with that hush and gentleness with which   We ever speak to a departing soul--
'**Brother! the blood of Jesus Christ, God's Son,   Cleanseth from every sin.**'

The pale lips moved,   And gently whispered 'hush!' and then they closed, And life again seemed gone.

But yet once more   They whispered those thrice blessed words, in hope To point the parting soul to Christ and heaven--   '**Brother! the precious blood of Jesus Christ   Can cleanse from every sin.**'

Again the pale lips moved,   All else was still and motionless, for Death Already had his fatal work half done;   But gathering up his quickly failing strength, The dying soldier--dying victor--said: 'Hush! for the angels call the muster roll!   I wait to hear my name!'

They spoke no more.   What need to speak again? for now full well They knew on whom his dying hopes were fixed,   And what his prospects were. So, hushed and still,   They, kneeling, watched.

And presently a smile,   As of most thrilling and intense delight,   Played for a moment on the soldier's face,   And with his one last breath he whispered 'Here!'

'*I have sinned! What shall I do?*' cries this despairing soul at the beginning of my Bible.

'*The blood of Jesus Christ, His Son, cleanseth us from all sin!*' answers the man who leaned upon the Saviour's breast and gazed full into the thorn-crowned face of the Crucified.

'*That is what I want!*' exclaims the man at Malabar, speaking, not for himself alone, but for each and all of us.

'*Those words are more golden than gold!*' says Miss Havergal, as she orders them to be inscribed upon her tomb.

'*They are like a gleam from the Mercy-seat!*' cries Donald Menzies.

'*They are the sheet-anchor of my soul!*' Hedley Vicars tells his sweetheart. And he is a very wise man who, in the straits of his experience, stakes his faith upon that which such witnesses have tested and have found sublimely true.

XV
SILAS WRIGHT'S TEXT

I

Silas Wright was deprived by sheer modesty of the honor of being President of the United States. His is one of the truly Homeric figures in American history. By downright purity of motive, transparency of purpose, and the devotion of commanding powers to the public good, he won for himself the honor, the love and the unbounded confidence of all his fellows. It used to be said of him that he was as honest as any man under heaven *or in it*. He might have aspired to any office to which it was in America's power to call him. Only his extreme humility, and his dread of impeding the promotion of his friends, kept him from rising to a position in which his name would have taken its place with those of Washington and Lincoln. But he refused almost every honor. 'He refused cabinet appointments,' says Benton, in his ***Thirty Years' View***. 'He refused a seat on the bench of the Supreme Court of the United States; he rejected instantly the nomination of 1844 for Vice-President; he refused to be nominated for the Presidency. He spent as much time in declining office as others did in winning it. The offices he did accept were thrust upon him. He was born great and above office and unwillingly descended to it.' Whittier is very conservative in his choice of heroes. Those whom he commemorates in verse are not only great men, but good ones. And Silas Wright is among them. 'Man of the millions,' he says, in the lines that he penned on hearing of Mr. Wright's death:

Man of the millions, thou art lost too soon!   Portents at which the bravest stand aghast--   The birththroes of a Future, strange and vast,   Alarm the land; yet thou, so wise, and strong,   Suddenly summoned to the burial bed,   Lapped in its slumbers deep and ever long,   Hear'st not the tumult surging overhead.   Who now shall rally Freedom's scattered host?   Who wear the mantle of the leader lost?

The splendid personality of Silas Wright has been best revealed to us in Irving Bacheller's ***The Light in the Clearing***. The book is partly history and partly commentary and partly fiction. Silas Wright, says Irving Bacheller, carried the candle of the Lord; and all the world rejoiced in its radiance.

II

Barton Baynes, the hero of the book--for whose actuality and historicity the author vouches--is an orphan brought up on a farm by his Uncle Peabody and Aunt Deel. Getting into all sorts of scrapes, he makes up his mind that he is too heavy a burden on the affectionate and good-natured couple; and one night he runs away. Out in the darkness, however, he meets with strange adventures, loses his way, and at length finds himself in the hands of Silas Wright, the Comptroller. The Senator first falls in love with the bright-faced, open-hearted, intelligent boy, and then takes him back to his uncle's farm. From that moment the friendship between the two--the great man and the obscure country boy--grows apace. After a while the Senator visits the district to deliver an address, and he spends the night at the farmhouse. It is a great occasion for Bart; and after supper an incident occurs that colors all his life and strikes the keynote of the book. As Barton approaches Mr. Wright to say Good-night, the Senator says:

'I shall be gone when you are up in the morning. It may be a long time before I see you; I shall leave something for you in a sealed envelope with your name on it. You are not to open the envelope until you go away to school. I know how you will feel that first day. When night falls, you will think of your aunt and uncle and be very lonely. When you go to your room for the night I want you to sit down all by yourself and read what I shall write. They will be, I think, the most impressive words ever written. You will think them over, but you will not understand them for a long time. Ask every wise man you meet to explain them to you, for all your happiness will depend upon your understanding of those few words in the envelope.'

The words in the sealed envelope!

What are the mysterious words in the envelope?

And what if the sealed envelope contains a *text*?

III

In the morning, when Barton rose, the Senator was gone, and Aunt Deel handed the boy the sealed envelope. It was addressed: 'Master Barton Baynes; to be opened when he leaves home to go to school.' That day soon came. At the Canton Academy, under the care of the excellent Michael Hacket, Bart felt terribly lonely, and, in accordance with the Senator's instructions, he opened the note. And this is what he read:

'Dear Bart, I want you to ask the wisest man you know to explain these words to you. I suggest that you commit them to memory and think often of their meaning. They are from Job: "***His bones are full of the sin of his youth, which shall lie down with him in the dust.***" I believe that they are the most impressive in all the literature I have read.--Silas Wright.'

Bart soon learned to love and admire the schoolmaster; *he* was the wisest man he knew; to *him*, therefore, he went for an explanation of the words.

'All true!' exclaimed Mr. Hacket, after reading the note. 'I have seen it sinking into the bones of the young, and I have seen it lying down with the aged in the dust of their graves. Your body is like a sponge; it takes things in and holds them and feeds upon them. A part of every apple that you eat sinks down into your blood and bones. You can't get it out. It's the same with the books that you read and the thoughts that you enjoy. They go down into your bones and you can't get them out. ***A man's bones are full of the sin of his youth, which lies down with him in the dust!***'

IV

But the best exposition of the text is not Michael Hacket's, but Irving Bacheller's. The whole book is a vivid and arresting and terrible forth-setting of the impressive words that Barton found in his sealed envelope.

All through the book two dreadful characters move side by side--Benjamin Grimshaw and Silent Kate. Benjamin Grimshaw is rich and proud and pitiless. Everybody is afraid of him. But Roving Kate is not afraid. Indeed, he seems to be more afraid of her. Wherever he is, she is there. She is wild and bony and ragged. She is, or pretends to be, half demented. She tells fortunes with strange antics and gesticulations, scrawling her prognostications upon stray slips of paper. But Benjamin Grimshaw is the main object of her attention. She hates him, and hates him all the more terribly because she once loved him. For Roving Kate, the Silent Woman, was once Kate Fullerton, Squire Fullerton's pretty daughter. And Benjamin Grimshaw had loved her, and betrayed her, and spurned her, and married another. In the village cemetery you might have seen a tombstone bearing her name. Her father erected it to show that she was dead ***to him*** for ever. Poor Kate had never known her mother. And so, in the course of the story, Benjamin Grimshaw had two sons, only one of whom he recognized. For Kate Fullerton was the mother of the other. And, in her shame and her anger and her hate, Kate resolved to follow the father of her base-born child all the days of his life; and there she stands--unkempt, repulsive, menacing--always near him, the living embodiment of ***the sin of his youth***.

Amos Grimshaw, his petted and pampered son, comes to the gallows. He is convicted of murder upon the highway. The father is in court when the Judge pronounces the awful sentence. And, of course, Roving Kate is there. Ragged as ever, the Silent Woman is waiting for him as he comes down the steps. She shoots out a bony finger at him, as, bowed and broken, he passes into the street. He turns and strikes at her with his cane.

'Go away from me,' he cries. 'Take her away, somebody! I can't stand it! She's killing me! Take her away!'

His face turns purple and then livid. He reels and falls headlong. He is dead!

Three days later they bury him. Roving Kate stands by the graveside, strangely changed. She is decently dressed; her hair is neatly combed; the wild look has left her eyes. She looks like one whose back is relieved of a heavy burden. She scatters little red squares of paper into the grave, her lips moving silently. These are her last curses. Barton Baynes and his schoolmaster, Mr. Hacket, are standing by.

'*The scarlet sins of his youth are lying down with him in the dust,*' whispers the master to his pupil as they walk away together.

V

This is terrible enough--the thought of our sins surrounding our deathbeds and lying down with us in our graves--but the book contains something more profound and terrible still!

For, in addition to the grave of Benjamin Grimshaw, from which we have just turned sadly away, there are two other graves in the book. The one is a felon's grave--the grave of Amos Grimshaw. And what sins are these that are lying down with him in the dust? They are some of them his own; and they are some of them his father's; and they are some of them the sins of Roving Kate, the Silent Woman. Yes, they are some of them the woman's sins. For when Amos was but an impressionable boy, Kate had supplied him with literature by which she hoped to pollute and ruin him.

Out of the deathless hatred that she bore to the father, she longed to destroy the son, body and soul. She gave him tales that would inflame his fancy and excite his baser instincts, tales that glorified robbery, murder and villainy of every kind. If Amos Grimshaw had been a good man's son, and if ennobling influences had been brought to bear upon him, he might have lived to old age and gone down at last to an honored grave. But his father's example was always before him, and Kate's books did their dreadful work only too well. He became a highway robber; he shot a stranger on a lonely road. It came out in evidence that the deed had been perpetrated under circumstances identical with those described in one of the sensational stories found in the Grimshaw barn--the stories Kate had given him!

'It's the same with the books you read,' the schoolmaster had said, when Bart sought from him an explanation of the text in the sealed envelope; 'they go down into your bones and you can't get them out.'

And Kate's books had gone down into Amos Grimshaw's bones; and thus her sins and his father's sins lay down in the dust of the felon's grave and mingled with his own. No exposition of Silas Wright's text could be more arresting or alarming than that. My sins may overflow from my grave and lie down in the dust with my children!

VI

And, on the very last page of *The Light in the Clearing*, we have an even more striking presentment of the same profound truth. For I said that, in the book, there is yet one other grave. It is a lonely grave up among the hills--the grave of the stranger who was shot by Amos Grimshaw that dark night; and this time it is old Kate who sits weeping beside it. For who was the stranger murdered upon the highway? It turns out to have been **Kate's own son**!

'It is very sorrowful,' she moans. 'He was trying to find me when he died!'

And so the murderer and the murdered were step-brothers! They were both the sons of Benjamin Grimshaw!

And, in this grave up among the hills, there lie down with poor murdered Enoch his own sins--whatever they may have been--and his father's sins--the sins that made him an outcast and a fugitive--and his mother's sins, the sins of the only being who loved him!

Yes, his mother's sins; for his mother's sins had slain him. In her hatred of Benjamin Grimshaw, she had moved Amos Grimshaw to become a murderer, and he had murdered--**her own son!**

'It is very sorrowful!' she moans.

It is indeed; sin is always sorrowful.

VII

'Wherefore come now and let us reason together, saith the Lord; though your sins be as scarlet, they shall be as white as snow; though they be red like crimson, they shall be as wool.'

It is best to make an end of them, and to turn from them, once and for all, that they lie down at last neither with us nor with our children.

XVI
MICHAEL FARADAY'S TEXT

I

The lecturer had vanished! A crowded gathering of distinguished scientists had been listening, spellbound, to the masterly expositions of Michael Faraday. For an hour he had held his brilliant audience enthralled as he had demonstrated the nature and properties of the magnet. And he had brought his lecture to a close with an experiment so novel, so bewildering and so triumphant that, for some time after he resumed his seat, the house rocked with enthusiastic applause. And then the Prince of Wales--afterwards King Edward the Seventh--rose to propose a motion of congratulation. The resolution, having been duly seconded, was carried with renewed thunders of applause. But the uproar was succeeded by a strange silence. The assembly waited for Faraday's reply; but the lecturer had vanished! What had become of him? Only two or three of his more intimate friends were in the secret. They knew that the great chemist was something more than a great chemist; he was a great Christian. He was an elder of a little Sandemanian Church--a church that never boasted more than twenty members. The hour at which Faraday concluded his lecture was the hour of the week-night prayer-meeting. That meeting he never neglected. And, under cover of the cheering and applause, the lecturer had slipped out of the crowded hall and hurried off to the little meeting-house where two or three had met together to renew their fellowship with God.

In that one incident the man stands revealed. All the sublimities and all the simplicities of life met in his soul. The master of all the sciences, he kept in his breast the heart of a little child. Mr. Cosmo Monkhouse has well asked--

> Was ever man so simple and so sage, So crowned and yet so careless of a prize? Great Faraday, who made the world so wise, And loved the labor better than the wage!
>
> And this, you say, is how he looked in age, With that strong brow and these great humble eyes That seem to look with reverent surprise On all outside himself. Turn o'er the page, Recording Angel, it is white as snow! Ah, God, a fitting messenger was he To show Thy mysteries to us below! Child as he came has he returned to Thee! Would he could come but once again to show The wonder-deep of his simplicity!

In him the simplicities were always stronger than the sublimities; the child outlived the sage. As he lay dying they tried to interview the professor, but it was the little child in him that answered them.

'What are your speculations?' they inquired.

'Speculations?' he asked, in wondering surprise. 'Speculations! I have none! I am resting on certainties. *I know whom I have believed and am persuaded that He is able to keep that which I have committed unto Him against that day!*' And, reveling like a little child in those cloudless simplicities, his great soul passed away.

II

Faraday was a perpetual mystery. He baffled all his colleagues and companions. Nobody could understand how the most learned man of his time could find in his faith those restful certainties on which he so calmly and securely reposed. They saw him pass from a meeting of the Royal Society to sit at the feet of a certain local preacher who was notorious for his illiteracy; and the spectacle filled them with bewilderment and wonder. Some suggested that he was, in an intellectual sense, living a double life. Tyndall said that, when Faraday opened the door of his oratory, he shut that of his laboratory. He did nothing of the kind. He never closed his eyes to any fragment of truth; he never divided his mind into watertight compartments; he never shrank from the approach of a doubt. He saw life whole. His biography has been written a dozen times; and each writer views it from a new angle. But in one respect they all agree. They agree that Michael Faraday was the most transparently honest soul that the realm of science has ever known. He moved for fifty years amidst the speculations of science whilst, in his soul, the certainties that cannot be shaken were singing their deathless song. Like a coastguard who, standing on some tall cliff, surveys the heaving waters, Faraday stood, with his feet upon the rock, looking out upon a restless sea of surmise and conjecture. In life, as in death, he rested his soul upon certainties. And if you will ask what those certainties were, his biographers will tell you that they were three.

1. *He trusted implicitly in the Father's love.* 'My faculties are slipping away day by day,' he wrote to his niece from his deathbed. 'Happy is it for all of us that our true good lies not in them. As they ebb, may they leave us as little children trusting in the Father of Mercies and accepting His unspeakable gift.'

2. *He trusted implicitly in the Redeeming Work of His Saviour.* 'The plan of salvation is so simple,' he wrote, 'that anyone can understand it--love to Christ springing from the love that He bears us, the love that led Him to undertake our salvation.'

3. *He trusted implicitly in the Written Word.* 'To complete this picture,' says Dr. Bence Jones, in bringing to a close his great two-volume biography, 'to complete this picture, I must add that Faraday's standard of duty was not founded upon any intuitive ideas of right and wrong, nor was it fashioned upon any outward experiences of time and place; but it was formed entirely on what he held to be the revelation of the will of God in the written Word, and throughout all his life his faith led him to act up to the very letter of it.'

'On these certainties,' he exclaimed, 'I stake everything! On these certainties I rest my soul!' And, summing up the three in one, he added, '*For I am persuaded that He is able to keep that which I have committed unto Him against that day.*'

It is wonderful how the universal heart aches for assurance, for confidence, for finality, for certainty. Mr. Dan Crawford tells of a cannibal chief beside whose deathbed an African boy was reading selections from the Gospel of John. He was impressed by the frequent recurrence of the words '*verily, verily.*'

'What do they mean?' he asked.

'They mean "*certainly, certainly!*"'

'Then,' exclaimed the dying man, with a sigh of infinite relief, 'they shall be my pillow. I rest on them.'

Sage or savage, it is all the same. Bunyan's great night was the night on which he found that same pillow. 'It was with joy that I told my wife, "O, now I know, *I know*!" That night was a good night to me! I never had a better. I longed for the company of some of God's people, that I might have imparted unto them what God had showed me. Christ was a precious Christ to my soul that night; I could scarcely lie in my bed for joy and peace and triumph through Christ!'

'*Those words shall be my pillow!*' said the African chief.

'*Those words shall be my pillow!*' said the English scientist.

'*Those words shall be my pillow!*' cried John Bunyan.

'*For I am persuaded that He is able to keep that which I have committed unto Him against that day!*'

III

'*He is able to keep!*' That was the sublime confidence that won the heart of John Newton. It came to him in the form of a dream on his voyage home from Venice. I have told the story in full in *A Bunch of Everlastings*. 'It made,' he says, 'a very great impression upon me!' The same thought made an indelible impression upon the mind of Faraday, and he clung tenaciously to it at the last. '*He is able to keep*'--as a shepherd keeps his sheep. '*He is able to keep*'--as a sentry keeps the gate. '*He is able to keep*'--as the pilgrims kept the golden vessels on their journey to Jerusalem, both counting and weighing them before they set out from Babylon and again on their arrival at the Holy City. '*He is able to keep*'--as a banker keeps the treasure confided to his custody.

'*I know whom I have believed*,' says the margin of the Revised Version, '*and I am persuaded that He is able to guard my deposit against that day*.'

'*I know in whom my trust reposes*,' says Dr. Weymouth's translation, '*and I am confident that He has it in His power to keep what I have entrusted to Him safe until that day.'*

'*I know whom I have trusted,*' says Dr. Moffatt's version, '*and I am certain that He is able to keep what I have put into His hands till the Great Day.*'

He will guard my treasure!
He will honor my confidence!
He will hold my deposit!
I know! I know! I know!

IV

Faraday's text is an ill-used text. It is frequently mis-quoted. It occurred one day in the course of a theological lesson over which Rabbi Duncan was presiding.

'Repeat that passage!' said the Rabbi to the student who had just spoken.

'*I know in whom I have----*'

'My dear sir,' interrupted the Rabbi, 'you must never let even a preposition come between you and your Saviour!'

And when Dr. Alexander, of Princeton, was dying, a friend endeavored to fortify his faith by reciting some of the most familiar passages and promises. Presently he ventured upon the words:

'*I know in whom I have believed, and----*'

But the sick man raised his hand.

'No, no,' exclaimed the dying Principal, 'it is not "I know *in* whom" but "I know *whom*"; I cannot have even the little word "*in*" between me and Christ. *I know whom I have believed, and am persuaded that He is able to keep that which I have committed unto Him against that day!*'

John Oxenham has expressed the same thought with an accent and emphasis well worthy of the theme:

    Not What, but **Whom**, I do believe, *That*, in my darkest hour of need, Hath comfort that no mortal creed To mortal man may give.

    Not What but **Whom**. For Christ is more than all the creeds, And His full life of gentle deeds Shall all the creeds outlive.

Not What I do believe, but ***Whom***. ***Who*** walks beside me in the gloom? ***Who*** shares the burden wearisome? ***Who*** all the dim way doth illume, And bids me look beyond the tomb   The larger life to live?
 Not what I do believe, But ***Whom***! Not What, But ***Whom***!

It was a Person, a Living and Divine Person, of whom Faraday was so certain and on whom he rested so securely at the last.

V

Is there in all Scottish literature a more robust, more satisfying, or more lovable character than **Donal Grant**? Readers of George Macdonald will cherish the thought of Donal as long as they live. He was the child of the open air; his character was formed during long and lonely tramps on the wide moor and among the rugged mountains; it was strengthened and sweetened by communion with sheep and dogs and cattle, with stars and winds and stormy skies. He was disciplined by sharp suffering and bitter disappointments. And he became to all who knew him a tower of strength, a sure refuge, a strong city, and the shadow of a great rock in a weary land. As a shepherd-boy among the hills he learned to read his Greek Testament; and, later on, he became tutor at the Castle Graham. It was his business in life to instruct little Davie, the younger son of Lord Morven; and he had his own way of doing it.

'Davie,' he said one day, 'there is One who understands every boy, and understands each separate boy as well as if there were no other boy in the whole world.'

'Tell me who it is!' demanded Davie.

'That is what I have to ***teach*** you; mere ***telling*** is not much use. ***Telling*** is what makes people think they know when they do not, and makes them foolish.'

'Well, what is his name?'

'I will not tell you that just yet; for then you would think that you knew Him when you knew next to nothing about Him. Look here! Look at this book!' He pulled from his pocket a copy of Boethius. 'Look at the name on the back of it; it is the name of the man who wrote that book.'

Davie spelled it out.

'Now you know all about the book, don't you?'

'No, sir, I don't know anything about it.'

'Well, then, my father's name is Robert Grant; you know now what a good man he is!'

'No, I don't!' replied Davie.

And so Donal led Davie to see that to know ***the name*** of Jesus, and to know ***about*** Jesus is not to know ***Jesus***.

'I know ***Him***!' cried Faraday in triumph.

George Macdonald makes Faraday's text the master-passion of his hero's life to the last. All through the adventures recorded in the book, Donal Grant behaves like a man who is very sure of God. '***I know Him***,' he seems to say. '***I know Him.***' And the closing sentences of the story tell us that 'Donal is still a present power of heat and light in the town of Auchars. He wears the same solemn look, the same hovering smile. That look and that smile say to those who can read them, "***I know whom I have believed***." His life is hid with Christ in God; he has no anxiety about anything; God is, and all is well.'

VI

'***I know whom I have believed.***'

Pascal had the words engraved upon his seal; Canon Ainger left instructions that they should be inscribed on his tomb at Darley Abbey; but, like Donal Grant, Michael Faraday wove them into the very warp and woof, the fiber and fabric of his daily life.

'Speculations!' he cried in dismay, 'speculations! I have none! I am resting on certainties! ***For I know whom I have believed and am persuaded that He is able to keep that which I have committed unto Him against that day!***'

Happy the heads that, in the soul's last straits, find themselves pillowed serenely there!

XVII
JANET DEMPSTER'S TEXT

I

Sitting here in my pleasaunce on the lawn, surrounded by a riot of hollyhocks, foxgloves, roses, geraniums, and other English flowers that she described so vividly, and loved so well, I find myself celebrating in my own way the hundredth anniversary of the birth of George Eliot. Lying open beside me on the garden-seat is a very well-worn copy of ***Janet's Repentance***. It has been read many times, and must be read again to-day. For even those who cannot go as far as Dr. Marcus Dods in pronouncing it 'one of the greatest religious books ever written' will at least agree that in religious feeling, spiritual insight and evangelical intensity, it is among the most noble and most notable of our English classics. The pity of it is that, long before the book was written, its brilliant authoress had drifted away from that simple and majestic faith which she so tenderly portrays. Indeed, I have sometimes fancied that she wrote of Janet with a great wistfulness in her heart. She seems to have felt that if, in the straits of her soul, she had found her storm-tossed spirit in communion with personalities like those by whom Janet was surrounded in the day of her distress, her spiritual pilgrimage might have been a sunnier one. But she drifted. No other word will describe the process. Some powerful but sensitive minds, like that of Goethe--with whose works she was so familiar--have been driven or torn from their anchorage by some sudden and desolating calamity; but with George Eliot it was quite otherwise. She was a gentle English girl, born on a farm, and passionately attached to the quiet beauty of the countryside. She delighted in the village green, the rectory garden, the fields waving with golden buttercups, and the shady woods in which the primroses twinkled. She loved to watch the poppies tossing in the corn, the wind sweeping over the red sea of clover, and the hyacinths nodding on the banks of the silvery stream. The smell of the hay and the song of the birds and the life of the fields were her ceaseless satisfaction and refreshment. Perhaps, as she wandered about those winding lanes and lonely bridle-paths, she became too contemplative, too introspective, too much addicted to the analysis of frames and feelings. Perhaps, dwelling so exclusively on the abstract and the ideal, her fresh young spirit became unfitted for its rude impact with the actual and the real. Perhaps, too, she was unfortunate in respect of the particular specimens of the evangelical faith that came under her notice. Perhaps! At any rate, she came at length into daily contact with men and women, and her girlish faith reeled under the shock. It is one of the most grievous tragedies of the spiritual realm that conscience often finds the sunny climate of an ardent evangelism singularly enervating. The **emotional** side of one's nature luxuriates in an atmosphere in which the **ethical** side becomes languid and relaxed. A man must be very careful, as Mr. Gladstone once incisively observed, to prevent his religion from damaging his morality. The simpleminded people with whom this sharp-witted and fresh-spirited young Englishwoman met had not fortified themselves against that insidious peril. One woman told a lie and the offense was sheeted home to her. '***Ah, well,***' she replied, in a nonchalant and easy way, '***I do not feel that I have grieved the Spirit much!***' George Eliot was horrified. She saw, to her disgust, that strong religious feeling could consist with flagrant dishonor. Her finely poised and sensitive soul experienced a revolt and a rebound. She changed none of her opinions, yet she changed the entire attitude of her mind; and, with the passage of time, the new attitude produced new ideas. She had not quarreled with the faith of her childhood; she simply lost her love for it. Her anchor relinquished its hold, and, almost imperceptibly, she drifted. 'She glided out of the faith,' as Principal Fairbairn so expressively puts it, 'as easily and as softly as if she had been a ship obeying wind and tide, and her faith a sea that opened silently before and closed noiselessly behind her.'

Wherefore let all those who name the name of Christ depart from iniquity! For if, through any glaring inconsistency between my faith and my behavior, I offend one of these little ones that believe in Him, it were better, so the Master Himself declared, that a millstone were hanged about my neck and that I were cast into the depths of the sea.

II

Now, in the story that lies open on the garden-seat beside me, all the characters are very religious people. Yet they are divided sharply into two classes. There are the very religious people who are all the worse for their religion, and there are the very religious people who are all the better for it. Mr. Dempster is a very religious man. In the opening sentence of the story, the first sentence in the book, he acknowledges his indebtedness to his Creator. He is a very religious man--and a drunkard! Mr. Budd is also a very religious man. Indeed, he is warden at the Parish Church. 'He is a small, sleek-headed bachelor of five and forty, whose scandalous life has long furnished his more moral neighbors with an afterdinner joke.' But a very religious man is Mr. Budd! Mrs. Linnett is a very religious woman. She dotes on religious biography. 'On taking up the biography of a celebrated preacher, she immediately turns to the end to see what he died of,' and she likes the book all the better if a sinister element enters into its composition. Mrs. Linnett is a very religious woman--and a gossip! We are introduced to a whole group of such characters--men and women who are very religious, but who are none the better for their religion.

And, side by side with these unamiable figures, are a set of people, equally religious, whose characters are immeasurably sweetened and strengthened by their religion. It is not that they profess another faith, attend another church, or spend lives remote from the affairs with which the others have to do. As George Eliot herself pointed out, when the publisher hesitated to commit himself to this manuscript, it was not a case of one religion against another, or of one creed against another, or of one church against another, or even of one minister against another. The members of this second group move in the same environment as do the members of the first; Sunday by Sunday they make their way to the self-same sanctuaries; yet every day they grow in gentleness, in thoughtfulness, in kindness, and in all those graces of behavior that constitute the charm of lovable and helpful lives. In this attractive group we find Mr. Jerome, Mr. Tryan, and little Mrs. Pettifer.

It is, of course, an old story, vividly and startlingly retold. The same cause will produce diametrically opposite effects. The sun that softens the wax hardens the clay. The benefit that I derive from my religion, and the enjoyment that it affords me, must depend upon the response that I make to it. The rays of light that fade my coat add a warmer blush to the petals of the rose. Why? My coat does not want the light and makes no response to it; the rose cannot bloom without the light and drinks in the soft rays as the source of all its beauty. Under the influence of the sunshine, the violets in the vase droop and become noisome; the living lilies under my window unfold and assume an even statelier grace. It is all a matter of response. Religion was always beating upon the lives of Mr. Dempster and Mr. Budd and Mrs. Linnett, as the sunlight beats upon the coat and the cut-flowers. They did not open their hearts to it; they made no eager response to it; it was a thing that shone upon the surface, and that was all. Their lives consequently wilted and shriveled and grew less beautiful. They were like violets made vile by the very light that was designed to make them lovely. Mr. Tryan, Mr. Jerome and Mrs. Pettifer, on the other hand, opened their hearts to the love of God as the rose opens its petals to the light of the sun. Their religion was a revelry to them. So far from its merely beating upon the surface, as the sunlight beats upon the surface of the coat, it saturated the very depths of their being. They were like the lilies under my window; the rays that withered the violets in the vase only make *them* more graceful and more fair.

III

Here, then, are the two groups; and the central scene of the story is the transfer of the principal character from the one group to the other. Janet Dempster, the wife of Robert Dempster, is, like her husband, very religious, but, like him, she is none the better for her religion. But matters at home hurry to a climax. Dempster drinks more and more, and, drinking, goes from bad to worse. He treats his wife, first with coldness, and then with cruelty. At length comes the dreadful and dramatic scene that readers of the story will never erase from their memories. In a fit of drunken savagery he burst into her room at midnight. He drags her from her bed; pushes her down the stairs and along the hall; and then, opening the front door, he hurls her by sheer brute force out into the street. Here is George Eliot's picture: '***The stony street; the bitter north-east wind and darkness; and in the midst of them a tender woman thrust out from her husband's home in her thin nightdress, the harsh wind cutting her naked feet and driving her long hair away from her half-clad bosom, where the poor heart is crushed with anguish and despair.***' It is in these desperate straits that religion presents itself to her view in an entirely fresh guise.

In her extremity, poor Janet thinks of little Mrs. Pettifer--a member of that other group, the group that resembles the lilies under my window, the group of kindly souls whose lives have been irradiated and beautified by their faith. She taps at the cottage window; Mrs. Pettifer hastens to the door; and, as soon as that frightened little body can recover from the first shock of her astonishment, she draws Janet into the room and then into the warm bed. Having composed and soothed her, she slips out of bed again, lights the fire and makes a cup of tea. In ***this*** guise, religion presents itself to Janet!

But she needs more! A roof to shelter her, a fire to warm her and a friend to caress and mother her--these are very welcome; but her heart is crying out with a yet deeper hunger. She feels that she, a poor weak woman, is standing against a world that is too hard and too strong and too terrible for her. What can she do? Where can she go? Little Mrs. Pettifer urges her to open her heart to Mr. Tryan, the minister; and to Mr. Tryan she accordingly goes. And in Mr. Tryan she finds ready helpfulness, warm sympathy, and a perfect understanding of her inmost need. Her life, she feels, is but a tangled skein. To convince her that he is no stranger to such conditions, Mr. Tryan tells her of his own struggles and distresses. He has not stood aloof from the battle, looking on; he has been in the thick of the fight--***and has been wounded***. She feels for him, and, in feeling for him, becomes conscious that the healing of her own hurt has already begun. In ***this*** guise, religion presents itself to Janet Dempster!

In the person of Mrs. Pettifer and in the person of Mr. Tryan, religion became incarnate under the eyes of poor Janet. In the person of Mrs. Pettifer and in the person of Mr. Tryan, '***the word became flesh.***'

But Janet still needs more! Mrs. Pettifer shelters and soothes her ***body***; Mr. Tryan comforts and strengthens her ***mind***; but her ***soul***, her very ***self***, what is she to do with *that*? She feels that she cannot trust *herself* with *herself*. Is there no still greater incarnation of the faith?

Mrs. Pettifer is the ***Incarnation Motherly***.

Mr. Tryan is the ***Incarnation Ministerial***.

But, in her heart of hearts, there is still a deep and bitter cry. Mrs. Pettifer can comfort; she cannot keep through all the days to come! Mr. Tryan can counsel; he cannot guard from future sins and sorrows! To whom can she commit herself? It is from Mr. Tryan's lips that the answer comes. The words fall upon her broken spirit, as she herself tells us, like rain upon the mown grass:

'*COME UNTO ME, ALL YE THAT LABOR AND ARE HEAVY-LADEN, AND I WILL GIVE YOU REST!*'

And once more the solution is an incarnation! When Janet's storm-beaten ***body*** needed fire and food and shelter, religion became incarnate in the person of Mrs. Pettifer. When Janet's distracted ***mind*** needed counsel and guidance, religion became incarnate in the person of Mr. Tryan. But when Janet's sin-laden ***soul*** cried out for a Saviour Who could deliver her from the stains of the past, and keep her amidst the perils of the future, religion became incarnate in the Person of the Son of God!

The Incarnation Motherly!

The Incarnation Ministerial!

The Incarnation Mediatorial!

'*Come unto Me!*' the Saviour said. And Janet came! She was a changed woman! '*A delicious hope,*' George Eliot tells us, '***the hope of purification and inward peace, had entered into Janet's soul, and made it spring-time there as well as in the outer world!***' '***She felt,***' we are told again, '***like a little child whose hand is firmly grasped by its father, as its frail limbs make their way over the rough ground: if it should stumble, the father will not let it go.***' She had opened her heart to the living Lord as the living flowers open their petals to the glad sunlight; and He had become the strength of her life and her portion for ever. Temptation came, fierce and sudden and terrible; but He was always there and always able to deliver.

IV

In the correspondence with her publisher as to whether or not the manuscript should be printed, George Eliot assures him that the characters are drawn from life. And, in the closing paragraph of the story, she tells us that Janet--an old woman whose once-black hair is now quite gray--is living still. But Mr. Tryan, she says, is dead; and she describes the simple gravestone in Milby churchyard. '*But*,' she adds, '*there is another memorial of Edgar Tryan, which bears a fuller record; it is Janet Dempster, rescued from self-despair, strengthened with Divine hopes, and now looking back on years of purity and helpful labor. The man who has left such a memorial behind him must have been one whose heart beat with true compassion and whose lips were moved by fervent faith.*' It is the last sentence in the book; and every minister, as he closes the covers and lays it aside, will covet for himself some such incarnate monument. Only as a preacher's preaching is '*made flesh*' in that way, will it be understood and appreciated by the generations following.

XVIII
CATHERINE BOOTH'S TEXT

I

Who that was in London on October 14, 1890, can forget the extraordinary scenes that marked the funeral of Catherine Booth? It was a day of universal grief. The whole nation mourned. For Mrs. Booth was one of the most striking personalities, and one of the mightiest spiritual forces, of the nineteenth century. To the piety of a Saint Teresa she added the passion of a Josephine Butler, the purposefulness of an Elizabeth Fry, and the practical sagacity of a Frances Willard. The greatest in the land revered her, trusted her, consulted her, deferred to her. The letters that passed between Catherine Booth and Queen Victoria are among the most remarkable documents in the literature of correspondence. Mr. Gladstone attached the greatest weight to her judgment and convictions. Bishop Lightfoot, one of the most distinguished scholars of his time, has testified to the powerful influence which she exerted over him. And, whilst the loftiest among men honored her, the lowliest loved her.

Such strong lives have their secrets. Mrs. Booth had hers. Her secret was a text. As a child she learned it by heart; as a girl she pinned her faith to the promise it enshrined; amidst the stress and strain of a stormy and eventful life she trusted it implicitly; and, with all the tenacity of her keen, clear intellect, she clung to it at the last. In the standard **Life of Catherine Booth**--a huge work of a thousand pages--four chapters are devoted to the scenes at the deathbed. And then we read:

'The lips moved as though desiring to speak. Unable, however, to do so, the dying woman pointed to a wall-text, which had for a long time been placed opposite to her, so that her eyes could rest upon it.

MY GRACE IS SUFFICIENT FOR THEE

It was taken down and placed near her on the bed. But it was no longer needed. The promise had been completely fulfilled.'

'That,' said a speaker at one of the great Memorial Meetings in London, some of which were attended by many thousand people, 'that was her text!' And, as so often happens, her text explains her character.

For, considered apart from the text, the character is an insoluble enigma. It is like a consequence without a cause. I was talking a week or two ago with an old man, who, in Australia's earlier days, did a good deal of pioneering in the heart of the bush.

'Once,' he told me, 'soon after I first came out, I really thought that I had reached the end of everything. I was hopelessly lost. My strength was utterly exhausted. I had gone as far as I could go. The country around me was flat and dry; my thirst was a perfect agony; and my poor dog followed at my heels, her tongue hanging out, and her sides panting pitifully. We had not seen water for several days. I sat down under a great gum-tree, hoping that an hour's rest would bring me fresh heart and new vigor. I must have fallen asleep. When I awoke, Fan was standing near me, wagging her tail. She seemed contented and satisfied; her tongue no longer protruded. An hour or two later, I suddenly missed her; she had vanished in the scrub. She was away about twenty minutes. I determined to watch her. Presently she set out again, and I followed. Surely enough, she had found a tiny spring in a slight hollow about half a mile away; and by that spring we were saved.'

I have seen something like this in a higher realm. I recall, for example, Richard Cecil's story of his conversion. Richard Cecil--the friend and biographer of John Newton--was one of the great evangelical forces of the ***eighteenth*** century, as Catherine Booth was of the ***nineteenth***. But, in his early days, Richard Cecil was a skeptic. He called himself an infidel, but he was honest in his infidelity. He could face facts; and the man who can look facts fairly in the face is not far from the kingdom of God. Richard Cecil was not, his skepticism notwithstanding. 'I see,' he says, in telling us of the line of thought that he pursued as he lay in bed one night, 'I see two unquestionable facts.' And what were they? They both concerned his mother.

'*First*, my mother is greatly afflicted in circumstances, body and mind; and I see that she cheerfully bears up under all her suffering by the support that she derives from constantly retiring to her quiet room and her Bible.

'*Second*, my mother has a secret spring of comfort of which I know nothing; while I, who give an unbounded loose to my appetites, and seek pleasure by every means, seldom or never find it. If, however, there is any such secret in religion, why may I not attain to it as well as my mother? I will immediately seek it!'

He did; and those who are familiar with his life-story know of the triumphant result of that quest. It was precisely so with Mrs. Booth. Her children knew that, like the bushman's collie, she found refreshment at some secret spring. Later on, she told them of the text and led them, one by one, to the fountains of grace. '*My grace is sufficient for thee.*' And when, at last, the avenues of speech and hearing were closed, they hung the golden words before her clouding eyes. Again she greeted them with rapture, and, with unwavering confidence, pointed her children to their deathless message.

II

In his **Grace Abounding**, John Bunyan tells us that there was a period in his spiritual history when his soul was like a pair of scales. It partook of three phases. At one time the right-hand balance was down and the left-hand empty and high; then for awhile they were exactly and evenly poised; and, at the last, the left-hand balance dropped and that on the right-hand was swinging in the air.

At the *first* of these stages he was being tormented about the unpardonable sin. He reminded himself that, for Esau, there was no place for repentance; and he felt that there was none for him. The scale in which he laid his despair was heavily weighted; the scale in which he placed his hope was empty!

And the *second* stage--the stage that leveled the balances? 'One morning,' he says, 'as I was at prayer, and trembling with fear, lest there should be no word of God to help me, that piece of a sentence darted in upon me: ***My grace is sufficient!*** At this I felt some stay as if there might yet be hope. About a fortnight before, I had been looking at this very scripture, but I then thought that it could bring me no comfort, and I threw down the book in a pet. I thought that the grace was not large enough for me! no, not large enough! But now it was as if the arms of grace were so wide that they could enclose not only me but many more besides. And so *this* about the sufficiency of grace and *that* about Esau finding no place for repentance would be like a pair of scales within my mind. Sometimes one end would be uppermost and sometimes again the other; according to which would be my peace or trouble.'

And the *third* stage--the triumphant stage? Bunyan felt that the scales were merely level because, in the balance that contained the hope, he had thrown only four of the six words that make up the text. '*My grace is sufficient*'; he had no doubt about that, and it gave him encouragement. But '*for thee*'; he felt that, if only he could add those words to the others, it would turn the scales completely. 'I had hope,' he says, 'yet because the "*for thee*" was left out, I was not contented, but prayed to God for *that* also. Wherefore, one day, when I was in a meeting of God's people, full of sadness and terror, these words did with great power suddenly break in upon me; *My grace is sufficient for thee, My grace is sufficient for thee, My grace is sufficient for thee*, three times together. And oh! methought that every word was a mighty word unto me; as *My* and *grace*, and *sufficient*, and *for thee*; they were then, and sometimes are still, far bigger than all others. Then, at last, that about Esau finding no place for repentance began to wax weak and withdraw and vanish, and this about the sufficiency of grace prevailed with peace and joy.' And so the issue was reversed; the scale that held the hope overweighed completely the scale that held the despair.

If it were not that others have passed through an identically similar experience, we should feel inclined to marvel at Bunyan's reluctance to cast into the balances the tail of the text: *My grace is sufficient--for thee!* It seems strange, I say, that Bunyan should have grasped with such confidence the *four* words and then boggled at the other *two*. And yet it is always easier to believe that there is a Saviour for the world than to believe that there is a Saviour *for me*. It is easy to believe that

There is grace enough for thousands   Of new worlds as great as this;   There is room for fresh creations   In that upper home of bliss;

but it is much harder to believe that there is grace and room *for me*. Martin

Luther believed implicitly and preached confidently that Christ died for all mankind, long before he could persuade himself that Christ died for Martin Luther. John Wesley crossed the Atlantic that he might proclaim the forgiveness of sins to the Indians; but it was not until he was verging upon middle life that he realized the possibility of the forgiveness of his own.

It is all very illogical, of course, and very absurd. If we can accept the *four* words, why not accept all *six*? If we credit the head of the text, why cavil at the tail? Sometimes the absurdity of such irrational behavior will break upon a man and set him laughing at his own stupidity. Mr. Spurgeon had some such experience. 'Gentlemen,' he said, one Friday afternoon, in an address to his students, 'Gentlemen, there are many passages of Scripture which you will never understand until some trying or singular experience shall interpret them to you. The other evening I was riding home after a heavy day's work; I was very wearied and sore depressed; and, swiftly and suddenly as a lightning flash, that text laid hold on me: ***My grace is sufficient for thee!*** On reaching home, I looked it up in the original, and at last it came to me in this way. ***MY grace is sufficient for THEE***! "Why," I said to myself, "I should think it is!" and I burst out laughing. I never fully understood what the holy laughter of Abraham was like until then. It seemed to make unbelief so absurd. It was as though some little fish, being very thirsty, was troubled about drinking the river dry; and Father Thames said: "Drink away, little fish, my stream is sufficient for thee!" Or as if a little mouse in the granaries of Egypt, after seven years of plenty, feared lest it should die of famine, and Joseph said: "Cheer up, little mouse, my granaries are sufficient for thee!" Again I imagined a man away up yonder on the mountain saying to himself: "I fear I shall exhaust all the oxygen in the atmosphere." But the earth cries: "Breathe away, O man, and fill thy lungs; my atmosphere is sufficient for thee!"' John Bunyan enjoyed a moment's merriment of the same kind when he threw the last two words into the scale and saw his despair dwindle into insignificance on the instant.

III

Some such thought shines through the passage in which Paul tells us how the great words came to him. He was irritated by his thorn; he prayed repeatedly for its removal; but the only answer that he received was this: ***My grace is sufficient for thee!*** Grace sufficient for a thorn! It is an almost ludicrous association of ideas!

It is so easy for Bunyan to believe that the divine grace is sufficient for the wide, wide world; it is so difficult to realize that it is sufficient for him!

It is so easy for Wesley to believe in the forgiveness of sins: it is so difficult for him to believe in the forgiveness of his own!

It is so easy for Paul to believe in the grace that is sufficient to redeem a fallen race: it is so difficult for him to believe in the grace that can fortify him to endure his thorn!

And yet, in a fine essay on **Great Principles and Small Duties**, Dr. James Martineau has shown that it is the lowliest who most need the loftiest; it is the tiny thorn that calls for the most tremendous grace. The gravest mistake ever made by educationalists is, he says, the mistake of supposing that those who know little are good enough to teach those who know less. It is a tragedy, he declares, when the master is only one stage ahead of his pupil. 'The ripest scholarship,' he maintains, 'is alone qualified to instruct the most complete ignorance.' Dr. Martineau goes on to show that a soul occupied with great ideas best performs trivial duties. And, coming to the supreme example of his subject, he points out that 'it was the peculiarity of the Saviour's greatness, not that he stooped to the lowliest, but that, without stooping, he penetrated to the humblest wants. He not simply stepped aside to look at the most ignominious sorrows, but went directly to them, and lived wholly in them; scattered glorious miracles and sacred truths along the hidden by-paths and in the mean recesses of existence; serving the mendicant and the widow, blessing the child, healing the leprosy of body and of soul, and kneeling to wash even the traitor's feet.' Here is a strange and marvelous and beautiful law! The loftiest for the lowliest! The greatest grace for the tiniest thorn!

Is it any wonder that, this being so, Paul felt that his splinter positively shone? '***I will glory in it***,' he cried, '***that the power of Christ may be billeted upon me.***' He feels that his soul is like some rural hamlet into which a powerful regiment has marched. Every bed and barn is occupied by the soldiers. Who would not be irritated by a splinter, he asks, if the irritation leads to such an inrush of divine power and grace? It is like the pain of the oyster that is healed by a pearl.

And so, with Paul as with Bunyan, the grace turns the scales. It is better to have the pain if it brings the pearl. It is better to have a thorn in the one balance if it brings such grace into the opposite balance that one is better off **with** the thorn than **without** it. Therein lies life's deepest secret--the secret that Catherine Booth and John Bunyan learned from the lips that unfolded it to Paul. In ***The Master's Violin***, Myrtle Reed tells us the secret of the music that the old man's fingers wooed from the Cremona. You have but to look at the master, she says, and you will comprehend. 'There he stands, a stately figure, gray and rugged, yet with a certain graciousness; simple, kindly, and yet austere; one who had accepted his sorrow, and, by some alchemy of the spirit, transmuted it into universal compassion, to speak, through the Cremona, to all who could understand!'

That is the secret--the old musician's secret; Catherine Booth's secret; Bunyan's secret; Paul's secret; the secret of all who have learned the text ***by heart***!

My grace is sufficient for thee--the inrush of the grace turned Paul's torturing splinter into a cause for life-long thankfulness!

My grace is sufficient for thee--the inrush of the grace turned Mrs. Booth's fierce struggle into a ceaseless song!

My grace is sufficient for thee! To the man who like John Bunyan, stands weighing his gladnesses and sadnesses with that text in his mind, it will seem that the one scale is overflowing and the other empty. For it is the glory of the grace that it takes what sadnesses there are and transmutes them into songs sublime.

XIX
UNCLE TOM'S TEXT

I

Poor old Uncle Tom has been stripped of everything. All that he counted precious has vanished. He has been torn away from the old Kentucky home; has been snatched away from the arms of old Aunt Chloe; has been sold away from children and kindred; and has fallen into the merciless hands of that vicious slave-dealer, Simon Legree. And now Uncle Tom is dying. He lies in the dusty shed, his back all torn and lacerated by the cruel thongs. All through the night there steal to his side the other slaves on the plantation, poor creatures who creep in to see the last of him, to bathe his wounds, to ask his pardon, or to kneel in prayer beside his tortured frame. With the morning light comes George Shelby, his old master, to redeem him.

'Is it possible, is it possible?' he exclaims, kneeling down by the old slave. 'Uncle Tom, my poor, poor old friend!'

But Uncle Tom is too far gone. He only murmurs faintly to himself:

Jesus can make a dying bed   Feel soft as downy pillows are.

'You shan't die; you mustn't die, nor think of it! I've come to buy you and take you home!' cries George, with impetuous vehemence.

'Oh, Mas'r George, ye're too late. The Lord's bought me and is going to take me home--and I long to go. Heaven is better than old Kentucky!'

At this moment the sudden flush of strength which the joy of meeting his young master had infused into the dying man gives way. A sudden sinking falls upon him; he closes his eyes; and that mysterious and sublime change passes over his face that suggests the approach of other worlds. He begins to draw his breath with long, deep inspirations, and his broad chest rises and falls heavily. The expression of his face is that of a conqueror.

'***Who***,' he murmurs, '***who--who--who shall separate us from the love of Christ?***' And, with that unanswerable challenge upon his quivering lips, he falls into his last long sleep. Severed from all that is dear to him, there is yet One heart from which nothing can separate him. And in that indissoluble tie he finds strong consolation at the last.

II

I was speaking the other day to a lady who had known Signor Alessandro Gavazzi. 'When he was in England,' she told me, 'he used to come and stay at my father's home, and, to us girls, he seemed like a visitor from another world.' The life of Gavazzi is one of the stirring romances of the nineteenth century. Born at Bologna in 1809, he became, at the age of fifteen, a Barnabite monk. His eloquence, even in his teens, was so extraordinary that, at twenty, he was made Professor of Rhetoric in the College of Naples. Some years afterward Pope Pius the Ninth sent him on a special mission to Milan as Chaplain-General to the Patriotic Legion. A little later, however, a new light broke upon him. He left the church of his fathers and devoted his distinguished gifts to the work of evangelism. In connection with his conversion, a pathetic incident occurred. A superstitious Italian mother will sometimes hang a charm around her boy's neck to drive away malignant powers. When Gavazzi was but a baby, his mother placed a locket on his breast, and he never moved without it. But when, in riper years, he found the Saviour, his mother's gift caused him great perplexity. As a charm he had no faith in it; he relied entirely on the grace of his Lord to sustain and protect him. And yet, for his mother's sake, he felt that he should like to wear it. He solved the problem by placing in the locket the words by which he had been led to Christ. When he died, an old man of eighty, the locket was found next his skin. And, when they opened it, they read: '***Who shall separate us from the love of Christ? I am persuaded that neither death, nor life, nor angels, nor principalities, nor powers, nor things present, nor things to come,*** *nor height, nor depth, nor any other creature, shall be able to separate us from the love of God, which is in Christ Jesus our Lord.*' Gavazzi's excommunication nearly broke his heart. He left Rome to wander in strange lands, the most frightful anathemas and maledictions ringing in his ears. He was an exile and an outcast, shuddering under the curse of the church that he had served so devotedly and so long. Yet, after all, what did it matter? He had found a love--the love of Christ--that he had never known before; and from that all-compensating love no power in church or state, in heaven or earth, in time or in eternity, had power to tear him.

III

One is tempted to continue in this strain. It would be pleasant to speak of Hugh Kennedy, of Savonarola, and of others who found life and grace and inspiration in the text on which poor Uncle Tom pillowed his dying head. The testimony of such witnesses is strangely fascinating; their name is legion; we may yet cite one or two of them before we close. Meanwhile, we must pay some attention to the words of which they speak so rapturously. And even to glance at them is to fall in love with them. They are among the most stately, the most splendid, in all literature. Macaulay, who read everything, once found himself in Scotland on a fast day. It was a new experience for him, and he did not altogether enjoy it. 'The place,' he said, 'had all the appearance of a Puritan Sunday. Every shop was shut and every church open. I heard the worst and longest sermon that I ever remember. Every sentence was repeated three or four times over, and nothing in any sentence deserved to be said once. I withdrew my attention and read the Epistle to the Romans. I was much struck by the eloquence and force of some passages, and made out the connection and argument of some others which had formerly seemed to me unmeaning. I enjoyed the "***Who shall separate us from the love of Christ?***" I know few things finer.'

The words constitute themselves the greatest challenge ever uttered. Poets and painters have gloried in the conception of Ajax, on his lonely rock, defying all the gods that be. But what is ***that*** compared with ***this***? In the passage whose sublimities awoke the enthusiasm of Macaulay, and delivered him from insufferable boredom,

Paul claims to have reached the limits of finality, and he hurls defiance at all the forces of futurity.

'Who shall separate us from the love of Christ? Death? Life? Angels? Principalities? Powers? Things Present? Things to Come? Height? Depth? Any fresh Creation? I am persuaded that none of them can separate us from the love of God which is in Christ Jesus our Lord.'

IV

Neither death nor life can do it. Not death--nor even life. Both are formidable forces; and Paul knew which was the more dangerous of the two.

So he died for his faith. That is fine--   More than most of us do.   But, say, can you add to that line   That he lived for it, too?

When Elizabeth came to the English throne, a number of men and women, who were awaiting martyrdom under Mary, were liberated. Animated by the spirit of Ridley and Latimer, they would have kissed the faggots and embraced the stake. Yet, in the years that followed, some of them lapsed into indifference, went the way of the world, and named the name of Christ no more. The ordeal of life proved more potent and more terrible than the ordeal of a fiery death.

Bunyan had learned that lesson. When he was in the depths of his despair, envying the beasts and birds about him, and tormenting himself with visions of hellfire, he went one day to hear a sermon on the love of Christ. To use his own words, his 'comforting time was come.' 'I began,' he says, 'to give place to the word which with power did over and over again make this joyful sound within my soul: "***Who shall separate me from the love of Christ?***" And with that my heart was filled full of comfort and hope, and I could believe that my sins would be forgiven me. Yea, I was so taken with the love and mercy of God that I remember that I could not tell how to contain till I got home; I thought I could have spoken of His love to the very crows that sat upon the ploughed lands before me. Surely I will not forget this forty years hence?'

Forty years hence! Forty years hence Bunyan was sleeping in his quiet grave in Bunhill Fields; and nobody who visits that familiar resting-place of his supposes for a moment that ***death*** has separated him from the love of Christ.

But ***life***! Life is a far more dangerous foe. 'The tempter,' Bunyan tells us, 'would come upon me with such discouragements as these: "You are very hot for mercy, but I will cool you. This frame shall not last. Many have been as hot as you for a spirit, but I have quenched their zeal." With this, several, who were fallen off, would be set before mine eyes. Then I would be afraid that I should fall away, too, but, thought I, I will watch and take care. "Though you do," said the tempter, "I shall be too hard for you. I will cool you insensibly, by degrees, by little and little. Continual rocking will lull a crying child to sleep. I shall have you cold before long!" These things,' Bunyan continues, 'brought me into great straits. I feared that time would wear from my mind my sense of the evil of sin, of the worth of heaven, and of my need of the blood of Christ.' But at that critical moment a text came to his help--Uncle Tom's text, Signor Gavazzi's text. '***What shall separate us from the love of Christ? For I am persuaded that neither death, nor life, nor angels, nor principalities, nor powers, nor things present, nor things to come, nor height, nor depth, nor any other creature shall be able to separate us from the love of God which is in Christ Jesus our Lord.***' 'That,' Bunyan says, 'was a good word to me.'

Death cannot do it!--that is good!

Life cannot do it!--that is better!

'And now I hoped,' says Bunyan, in concluding his narrative of this experience, 'now I hoped that long life would not destroy me nor make me miss of heaven.'

V

Paul dares the universe. He defies infinity. He summons, in pairs, all the powers that be, and glories in their impotence to dissolve the sacred tie that binds him to his Lord.

He calls ***Life and Death*** before him and dares them to do it!

He calls the ***Powers of this World*** and the ***Powers of Every Other***; none of them, he says, can do it!

He calls the ***Things of the Historic Present*** and the ***Developments of the***

Boundless Future. Whatever changes may come with the pageant of the ages, there is one dear relationship that nothing can ever affect!

He calls the ***Things in the Heights*** and the ***Things in the Depths***; but neither among angels nor devils can he discover any force that makes his faith to falter!

He surveys ***this Creation*** and he contemplates ***the Possibility of Others***; but it is with a smile of confidence and triumph.

'***For I am persuaded***,' he says, '***that neither death, nor life, nor angels, nor principalities, nor powers, nor things present, nor things to come, nor height, nor depth, nor any other creature shall be able to separate us from the love of God which is in Christ Jesus our Lord.***'

VI

The covenanters knew the value of Uncle Tom's text. Among the heroic records of Scotland's terrible ordeal, nothing is more impressive or affecting than the desperate way in which persecuted men and women clung with both hands to the golden hope enshrined in that majestic word. It was in a Scottish kirk that Macaulay discovered its splendor; but even Macaulay failed to see in it all that ***they*** saw.

It was a beautiful May morning when Major Windram rode into Wigton and demanded the surrender, to him and his soldiers, of two women who had been convicted of attending a conventicle. One of them was Margaret Wilson, a fair young girl of eighteen. She was condemned to be lashed to a stake at low tide in such a way that the rising waters would slowly overwhelm her. In hope of shaking her fidelity, and saving her life, it was ordained that her companion should be fastened to a stake a little farther out. 'It may be,' said her persecutors, 'that, as Mistress Margaret watches the waves go over the widow before her, she will relent!' The ruse, however, had the opposite effect. When Margaret saw the fortitude with which the elder woman yielded her soul to the incoming tide, she began to sing a paraphrase of the twenty-fifth Psalm, and those on the beach took up the strain. The soldiers angrily silenced them, and Margaret's mother, rushing into the waters, begged her to save her life by making the declaration that the authorities desired. But tantalized and tormented, she never flinched; and, as the waves lapped her face she was heard to repeat, again and again, the triumphant words: '*I am persuaded that neither death, nor life, nor angels, nor principalities, nor powers, nor things present, nor things to come, nor height, nor depth, nor any other creature, shall be able to separate us from the love of God which is in Christ Jesus our Lord.*'

As a representative of the **men** of that stern time, we may cite John Bruce. When that sturdy veteran, after a long life of faithful testimony and incessant suffering, lay dying, he beckoned his daughter to the chair beside his bed. He told her, in broken sentences and failing voice, of the goodness and mercy that had followed him all the days of his life; and then, pausing suddenly, he exclaimed: 'Hark, lass, the Master calls! Fetch the Buik!' She brought the Bible to his side. 'Turn,' he said, 'to the eighth of Romans and put my finger on these words: "*Who can separate us from the love of Christ? For I am persuaded that neither death, nor life, nor angels, nor principalities, nor powers, nor things present, nor things to come, nor height, nor depth, nor any other creature, shall be able to separate us from the love of God which is in Christ Jesus our Lord.*" Now,' he continued, as soon as she had found the place, 'put my finger on the words and hold it there!' And with his finger there, pointing even in death to the ground of all his confidence, the old man passed away.

VII

'*Who shall separate us from the love of Christ?*' asked Uncle Tom, with his last breath.

'Massa George sat fixed with solemn awe,' says Mrs. Beecher Stowe, in continuing the story. 'It seemed to him that the place was holy; and as he closed Tom's lifeless eyes, and rose to leave the dead, only one thought possessed him--What a thing it is to be a Christian!'

It is indeed!

XX
ANDREW BONAR'S TEXT

I

It is an old-fashioned Scottish kirk--and the Communion Sabbath. Everybody knows of the hush that brooded over a Scottish community a century ago whenever the Communion season came round. The entire population gave itself up to a period of holy awe and solemn gladness. As the day drew near, nothing else was thought about or spoken of. At the kirk itself, day after day was given up to preparatory exercises, fast-time sermons and the fencing of tables. In this old kirk, in which we this morning find ourselves, all these preliminaries are past. The young people who are presenting themselves for the first time have been duly examined by the grave and somber elders, and, having survived that fiery and searching ordeal, have received their tokens. And now everything is ready. The great day has actually come. The snowy cloths drape the pews; everything is in readiness for the solemn festival; the people come from far and near. But I am not concerned with those who, on this impressive and memorable occasion, throng around the table and partake of the sacred mysteries. For, at the back of the kirk, high up, is a cavernous and apparently empty old gallery, dark and dismal. Is it empty? What is that patch of paleness that I see up in the corner? Is it a face? It is! It is the grave and eager face of a small boy; a face overspread with awe and wonder as he gazes upon the affecting and impressive scene that is being enacted below. 'As a child,' said Dr. Bonar, many years afterwards, when addressing the little people of his own congregation, 'as a child I used to love to creep up into that old gallery on Communion Sabbaths. How I trembled as I climbed up the stairs! And how I shuddered when the minister entered and began the service! When I saw young people of my own acquaintance take the holy emblems for the first time, I wondered if, one great and beautiful day, I should myself be found among the communicants. But the thought always died in the moment of its birth. For I found in my heart so much that must keep me from the love of Christ. I thought, as I sat in the deep recesses of that gloomy old gallery, that I must purge my soul of all defilement, and cultivate all the graces of the faith, before I could hope for a place in the Kingdom of Christ or venture as a humble guest to His table. But oh, how I longed one day to be numbered among that happy company! I thought no privilege on earth could compare with that.'

II

A couple of entries in his diary will complete our preparation for the record of the day that changed his life. He is a youth of nineteen, staid and thoughtful, but full of life and merriment, and the popular center of a group of student friends.

May 3, 1829.--Great sorrow, because I am still out of Christ.

May 31, 1829.--My birthday is past and I am not born again.

Not every day, I fancy, do such entries find their way into the confidential journals of young people of nineteen.

III

God's flowers are all everlastings. The night may enfold them; the grass may conceal them; the snows may entomb them; but they are always there. They do not perish or fade. See how the principle works out in history! There is no more remarkable revival of religion in our national story than that represented by the Rise of the Puritans. The face of England was changed; everything was made anew. Then came the Restoration. Paradise was lost. Puritanism vanished as suddenly as it had arisen. But was it dead? Professor James Stalker, in a Centennial Lecture on Robert Murray McCheyne--a name that stands imperishably associated with that of

Andrew Bonar--says most emphatically that it was not. He shows how, like a forest fire, the movement swept across Europe, returning at last to the land in which it rose. When, with the Restoration, England relapsed into folly, it passed over into Holland, preparing for us, among other things, a new and better line of English kings. From Holland it passed into Germany, and, by means of the Moravian Brethren, produced the most amazing missionary movement of all time. From Germany it returned to England, giving us the Methodist Revival of the eighteenth century, a revival which, according to Lecky, alone saved England from the horrors of an industrial revolution. And from England it swept into Scotland, and kindled there such a revival of religion as has left an indelible impression upon Scottish life and character. It was in the sweep of that historic movement that the soul of Andrew Bonar was born.

IV

'It was in 1830,' he says, in a letter to his brother, written in his eighty-third year, 'it was in 1830 that I found the Saviour, or rather, that He found me, and laid me on His shoulders rejoicing.' And how did it all come about? It was a tranquil evening in the early autumn, and a Sabbath. There is always something conducive to contemplation about an autumn evening. When, one of these days, one of our philosophers gives us a **Psychology of the Seasons**, I shall confidently expect to find that the great majority of conversions take place in the autumn. At any rate, Andrew Bonar's did. As he looked out upon the world in the early morning, he saw the shrubs in the garden below him, and the furze on the moorland beyond, twinkling with the dew-drenched webs of innumerable spiders. In his walk to the church, and in a stroll across the fields in the afternoon, the hush of the earth, broken only by the lowing of cattle, the bleating of sheep and the rustle of the leaves that had already fallen, saturated his spirit. The world, he thought, had never looked so beautiful. The forest was a riot of russet and gold. The hedge-rows were bronze and purple and saffron. The soft and misty sunlight only accentuated the amber tints that marked the dying fern. In the evening, unable to shake off the pensive mood into which the day had thrown him, he reached down Guthrie's **Trial of a**

Saving Interest in Christ, and gave himself to serious thought. Was it in the pages of Guthrie's searching volume that he came upon the text, or did he, later on, lay down the book and take up his New Testament instead? I do not know. But, however that may have been, one great and glowing thought took complete possession of his soul. As the tide will sometimes rush suddenly up the sands, filling up every hollow and bearing away all the seaweed and driftwood that has been lying there so long, so one surging and overmastering word poured itself suddenly in upon his mind, bearing away with it the doubts and apprehensions that had tormented him for years. '***Of His fullness have we all received, and grace for grace.***' Then and there, he says, he began to have a secret joyful hope that he did really believe on the Lord Jesus. 'The fullness and freeness of the divine grace filled my heart; I did nothing but receive!'

'***Of His fullness have all we received!***'
'***His fullness filled my heart!***'
'***I did nothing but receive!***'

Forty-two years afterwards, at the age of sixty-two, he revisited that room and tried to recapture the holy ecstasy with which, so many years earlier, he had 'first realized a found Saviour.'

'***Grace for grace!***'

V

'***Of His fullness have all we received, and grace for grace!***'

I know a fair Australian city that nestles serenely at the foot of a tall and massive mountain. Half way up the slopes is the city's reservoir. In a glorious and evergreen valley it has been hollowed out of the rugged mountain-side. The virgin bush surrounds it on every hand; at its western extremity a graceful waterfall comes pouring down from the heights, mingling its silvery music with the songs of the birds around. It is the favorite haunt of gaily-colored kingfishers. Swallows skim hither and thither over its crystalline and placid surface; and, as if kissing their own reflections in the glass, they just touch the water as they flit across, creating circles that grow and grow until they reach the utmost edge. Like a giant who, conscious of his grandeur, loves to see his image in the mirror, the scarped and weather-beaten summit gazes sternly down from above and sees his splendors reproduced, and even enhanced, in the limpid depths below. Often, on a hot day, have I resorted to this sylvan retreat. At this altitude, how deliciously cool is the air; how icy cold the water! It has come pouring down the cataract from the melting snows above! For, strangely enough, the winter rains and the summer suns conspire to keep it always full. Far down the mountain-side I see the city, shimmering in the noonday heat. I think of its population, hot, tired and thirsty. And then it pleases me to reflect that every house down there at the mountain's foot is in direct communication with this vast basin of shining water. The people have but to stretch forth their hands and replenish their vessels again and again. This crystal reservoir far up the slopes is really a part of the furniture of each of those homes. Have not I myself been down there in the dust and heat on such a day as this? Have not I myself been parched and thirsty? And have I not thought wistfully of the reservoir far up the slopes? And have I not taken my glass and filled it and quaffed with relish the sweet and sparkling water? And have I not said to myself, as I thought of the familiar scene among the hills: 'Of its fullness have all we received, and water for water.'

'His fullness filled my heart!'
'I did nothing but receive!'
'Of His fullness have all we received, and grace for grace!'

VI

Yes, grace for grace! Grace for manhood following upon grace for youth! Grace for sickness following upon grace for health! Grace for sorrow following upon grace for joy! Grace for age following upon grace for maturity! Grace to die following upon grace to live! Of that fullness of which he first drank on that lovely autumn evening, he drank again and again and again, always with fresh delight and satisfaction.

Twenty-five years later, I find him saying that, 'if there is one thing for which I praise the Lord more than another it is this: that He opened my eyes to see that Christ pleases the Father to the full, and that ***this*** is the ground of my acceptance.'

Five years later still, he says that 'I have been many, many times unhappy for awhile, but have never seriously doubted my interest in the Lord Jesus.'

When he was fifty-four, his wife died, leaving him to bring up his young family as best he could. But '***grace for grace***.' A year or two later, I find him rejoicing that 'to-night both Isabella and Marjory came home speaking of their having been enabled to rest on Christ. What a joyful time it has been! I think, too, the young servant has found Christ. Blessed Lord, I have asked Thee often to remember Thy promise, and "when mother leaves thee, the Lord will take thee up." I have asked Thee to be a mother to my motherless children, and now, indeed, Thou hast given me my prayer. Praise, praise for evermore!'

On the fiftieth anniversary of that never-to-be-forgotten autumn evening, he records with gratitude the fact that, 'for fifty years the Lord has kept me within sight of the Cross.'

Ten years later still, now an old man of eighty, he declares that his Saviour has never once left him in the darkness all these years.

And, two years later, just before his death, he writes, 'it was sixty-two years ago that I found the Saviour, or, rather, that He found me; and I have never parted company with Him all these years. Christ the Saviour has been to me my true portion, my heaven begun; and my earnest prayer and desire for you and Mary and little Marjory will always be, that you may each find, not only all I ever found in Christ, but a hundredfold more, every year!'

Grace for grace!

Grace for the father and grace for the children!

Grace for the old man just about to die, and grace for the little child just learning how to live!

'*Of His fullness have all we received, and grace for grace!*'

VII

Yes, ***grace for grace***! Grace for the pulpit and grace for the pew!' For, through all these years, Andrew Bonar was a minister, and the text was the keynote of all his utterances.

Fullness! Fullness! Fullness!
Receive! Receive! Receive!
Grace for grace! Grace for grace!
'Of His fullness have all we received, and grace for grace!'

In his study there hung a text of two words. He had had it specially printed, for those two words expressed the abiding fullness on which he loved to dwell. '***Thou remainest!***' One day, we are told, a lady in great sorrow called to see him. But nothing that he said could comfort her. Then, suddenly, he saw a light come into her face. 'Say no more,' she said, 'I have found what I need!' and she pointed to the text: '***Thou remainest!***'

That was it! Come what will, He abides! Go who may, He remains! Amidst all the chances and changes of life, He perennially satisfies. Like the thirsty toilers in the city, I draw and draw again, and am each time refreshed and revived.

'His fullness fills my heart!'
'I do nothing but receive!'
'Of His fullness have all we received, and grace for grace!'

XXI
FRANCIS D'ASSISI'S TEXT

I

Oscar Wilde declares that, since Christ went to the cross, the world has produced only one genuine Christian, and his name is Francis d'Assisi. Certainly he is the one saint whom all the churches have agreed to canonize; the most vividly Christlike man who has ever submitted his character to the scrutiny of public criticism. His life, as Green says in his ***Short History of the English People***, his life falls like a stream of light athwart the darkness of the mediaeval ages. Matthew Arnold speaks of him as a figure of most magical potency and sweetness and charm. Francis called men back to Christ and brought Christ back to men. 'All Europe woke with a start,' Sabatier affirms, 'and whatever was best in humanity leaped to follow his footsteps.'

II

A blithe saint was Francis. He loved to laugh; he loved to sing; and he loved to hear the music of laughter and of song as it rippled from the lips of others. Every description that has come down to us lays stress on the sunshine that played about his lofty forehead and open countenance. The days came when, though still in the heyday of early manhood, his handsome figure was gaunt and wasted; his fine face furrowed with suffering and care; his virile strength exhausted by ceaseless toil, wearisome journeyings, and exacting ministries of many kinds. But, emaciated and worn, his face never for a moment lost its radiance. He greeted life with a cheer and took leave of it with a smile.

His youth was a frolic; his very sins were pleasant sins. His winsomeness drew to him the noblest youths and fairest maidens of Assisi. The lithe and graceful figure of Francis, with his dark, eloquent but sparkling eyes, his wealthy shock of jet black hair, his soft, rich, sonorous voice and his gay but faultless attire, was the soul and center of every youthful revel. He was, as Sir James Stephen says, foremost in every feat of arms, first in every triumph of scholarship, and the gayest figure in every festival. 'The brightest eyes in Assisi, dazzled by so many graces, and the most reverend brows there, acknowledging such early wisdom, were alike bent with admiration towards him; and all conspired to sustain his father's confidence that, in his person, the family name would rival the proudest and most splendid in Italy's illustrious past.' His bewitching personality, his rollicking gaiety, his brooding thoughtfulness, his dauntless courage and his courtly ways swept all men off their feet; he had but to lead and they instinctively followed; he commanded and they unquestionably obeyed. He was nick-named **the Flower of Assisi**. He loved to be happy and to make others happy. 'Yet,' as one Roman Catholic biographer remarks, 'he did not yet know where true happiness was to be found.' He was twenty-four when he made that sensational discovery. He found the source of true happiness in the last place in the world in which he would have thought of looking for it. He found it at the Cross! And, in perfect consistency with his youthful conduct, he spent the rest of his days--he died at forty-four--in pointing men to the Crucified. As a youth he had done his best to radiate laughter and song among all the young people of Assisi; it was therefore characteristic of him that, having discovered the fountain-head of all abiding satisfaction, he should make it the supreme object of his maturer years to share his sublime secret with the whole wide world.

III

London was a village in the time of Francis d'Assisi, and the baying of the wolves was the only sound heard in the forests that then covered the sites of our great modern cities. Whilst King John was signing Magna Carta, Francis was at Rome seeking recognition for his brotherhood of friars. It was the age of the Crusaders and the Troubadours. Yet, as I read the moving record of his great spiritual experience, I forget that I have invaded a period in which English history had scarcely begun. Francis has his affinities in every land and in every age. Francis died four hundred years before John Bunyan was born; yet, as I read Bunyan's description of Christian at the Cross, I seem to be perusing afresh the story of the conversion of Francis. The language fits exactly. Strike out the word 'Christian,' and substitute the word 'Francis,' and the passage could be transferred bodily from the ***Pilgrim's Progress*** to the ***Life of Francis d'Assisi***.

The conversion of Francis occurred five hundred years before Dr. Watts wrote his noble hymn, '***When I survey the wondrous Cross***'; yet, without knowing the words, Francis sang that song in his heart over and over and over again.

The conversion of Francis was effected six hundred years before the conversion of Mr. Spurgeon. Yet that conversion in the ruined church of St. Damian's in Italy is the very counterpart of that later conversion in the little chapel at Artillery Street, Colchester.

'Look!' cried the preacher at Colchester, 'look to Jesus! Look to Jesus!' 'I looked,' says Mr. Spurgeon; 'I looked and was saved!'

'Francis looked to the Crucified,' says his biographer. 'It was a look of faith; a look of love; a look that had all his soul in it; a look which did not attempt to analyze, but which was content to receive. He looked, and, looking, entered into life.'

You can take the sentences from the ***Life of Francis*** and transfer them to the ***Life of Spurgeon***, or vice versa, and they will fit their new environment with the most perfect historical accuracy.

IV

As, with your face towards Spello, you follow the windings of the Via Francesca, you will find the little church of St. Damian's on the slope of the hill outside the city walls. It is reached by a few minutes' walk over a stony path, shaded with olive-trees, amid odors of lavender and rosemary. 'Standing on the top of a hillock, the entire plain is visible through a curtain of cypresses and pines which seem to be trying to hide the humble hermitage and set up an ideal barrier between it and the world.' Francis was particularly fond of this wooded walk and of the sanctuary to which it led. In pensive moments, when it was more than usually evident to him that, with all his merriment, he had not yet discovered the fountain of true gladness, he turned his face this way.

The crucifix at St. Damian's--which is still preserved in the sacristy of Santa Chiara--has features peculiarly its own. It differs from other images of the kind: 'In most of the sanctuaries of the twelfth century, the Crucified One, frightfully lacerated, with bleeding wounds, appears to seek to inspire only grief and compunction; that of St. Damian, on the contrary, has an expression of unutterable calm and gentleness; instead of closing the eyelids in eternal surrender to the weight of suffering, it looks down in self-forgetfulness, and its pure, clear gaze says, not "**See how I suffer!**" but "**Come unto Me!**"'

That, at any rate, is what it said to Francis on that memorable day. With an empty and a hungry heart he kneeled before it. 'O Lord Jesus,' he cried, 'shed Thy light upon the darkness of my mind!' And then an extraordinary thing happened. The Saviour to whom he prayed was no longer an inanimate image; but a living Person! 'An answer seemed to come from the tender eyes that looked down on him from the Cross,' says Canon Adderley. 'Jesus heard his cry, and Francis accepted the dear Lord as his Saviour and Master. A real spiritual union took place between him and his Divine Lord. He took Him for better for worse, for richer for poorer, till death and after death, for ever.' 'This vision marks,' Sabatier says, 'the final triumph of Francis. His union with Christ is consummated; from this time he can exclaim with the mystics of every age, "My beloved is mine and I am His." From that day the remembrance of the Crucified One, the thought of the love which had triumphed in immolating itself, became the very center of his religious life, the soul of his soul. For the first time, Francis had been brought into direct, personal, intimate contact with Jesus Christ.' 'It was,' Canon Adderley says again, 'no mere intellectual acceptance of a theological proposition, but an actual self-committal to the Person of Jesus; no mere sentimental feeling of pity for the sufferings of Christ, or of comfort in the thought that, through those sufferings, he could secure a place in a future heaven, but a real, brave assumption of the Cross, an entering into the fellowship of the Passion of Christ, a determination to suffer with Him and to spend and be spent in His service.'

Francis never forgot that moment. His whole soul overflowed with the intensity of his affection for his Saviour. To the end of his days he could never think of the Cross without tears; yet he never knew whether those tears were prompted by admiration, pity, or desire.

When he arose and left the little sanctuary, he felt, as Bunyan's pilgrim felt, that he had lost his load, and lost it for ever.

But he felt that he had assumed another. He had taken up the Cross. He had devoted himself to its service. '***God forbid***,' he cried, '*that I should glory save in the Cross of our Lord Jesus Christ, by whom the world is crucified unto me and I unto the world.*' When, five centuries later, Isaac Watts surveyed the wondrous Cross on which the Prince of Glory died, his contemplation led to the same resolve:

Forbid it, Lord, that I should boast, Save in the death of Christ my God! All the vain things that charm me most, I sacrifice them to His blood.

And so, once more, without knowing the words, Francis sang in his soul that song of consecration.

'*I looked and looked and looked again!*' say Francis and Spurgeon, six centuries apart.

'*It was very surprising to me that the sight of the Cross should thus ease me of my burden!*' say Francis and Bunyan, with four centuries between.

'*Forbid it, Lord, that I should boast save in the death of Christ my God!*' cry Francis and Isaac Watts, undivided by a chasm of five hundred years.

In the presence of the Cross all the lands are united and all the ages seem as one.

V

'*God forbid that I should glory save in the Cross of our Lord Jesus Christ, by whom the world is crucified unto me and I unto the world.*' In the one cross Francis saw--as Paul did--three crucifixions.

He saw on the Cross ***his Lord crucified for him***.
He saw on the Cross ***the world crucified to him***.
He saw on the Cross ***himself crucified to the world***.

From that hour Francis knew nothing among men save Jesus Christ and Him crucified. Laying aside the gay clothing of which he was so fond, he donned a peasant's cloak and tied it at the waist with a piece of cord--the garb that afterwards became the habit of the Franciscan Order. He then set out to initiate the greatest religious revival and the greatest missionary movement of the mediaeval ages--the enterprise that paved the way for the Renaissance and the Reformation. Beginning at his native town, he journeyed through the classic cities of Italy, unfolding to all sorts and conditions of men the wonders of the Cross. Although the hideous sight and loathsome smell of leprosy had always filled him with unconquerable disgust, he gladly ministered to the lepers, in the hope that, by so doing, he might impart to them the infinite consolations of the Cross. Worn as he soon became, he set out to tramp from land to land in order that he might proclaim through Europe and Asia the matchless message of the Cross. In his walks through the lonely woods he loved to proclaim to the very birds the story of the Cross. It is another link with Bunyan. Bunyan felt that he should like to tell the crows on the ploughed fields the story of his soul's salvation; but Francis actually did it. He would sit down in the forest: wait until the oaks and beeches and elms about him were filled with sparrows and finches and wrens; and then tell of the dying love of Him who made them. And, as they flew away, he loved to fancy that they formed themselves into a cross-shaped cloud above him, and that the songs that they sang were the rapt expression of their adoring worship. In his long journeyings he was often compelled to subsist on roots and nuts and berries. Meeting a kindred spirit in the woods he one day suggested that they should commune together. His companion looked about him in bewilderment. But Francis pointed to a rock. 'See!' he said, 'the rock shall be our altar; the berries shall be our bread; the water in the hollow of the rock shall be our wine!' It took very little to turn the thoughts of Francis to the Cross; he easily lifted his soul into communion with the Crucified. Whenever and wherever Francis opened his lips, the Cross was always his theme. 'He poured into my heart the sweetness of Christ!' said his most eminent convert, and thousands could have said the same. Feeling the magnitude of his task and the meagerness of his powers, he called upon his converts to assist him, and sent them out, two by two, to tell of the ineffable grace of the Cross. In humanness and common sense he founded his famous Order. His followers were to respect domestic ties; they were to regard all work as honorable, and to return an equivalent in labor for all that they received. They were to husband their own powers; to regard their bodies as sacred, and on no account to exhaust their energies in needless vigils and fastings. The grey friars soon became familiar figures in every town in Europe. They endured every conceivable privation and dared every form of danger in order that, like their founder, they might tell of the deathless love of the Cross.

Francis himself did not live long to lead them; but in death as in life his eyes were on the Cross. Fifty of his disciples knelt around his bed at the last. He begged them to read to him the 19th chapter of John's gospel--the record of the Crucifixion. 'In living or in dying,' he said, '**God forbid that I should glory save in the Cross of our Lord Jesus Christ!**'

VI

Francis d'Assisi and Matthew Arnold appear to have little or nothing in common. Francis was emotional, mystical, seraphic; Arnold was cultured, cold, and critical. Yet Francis threw an extraordinary spell over the scholarly mind of Arnold, and, dissimilar as were their lives, in death they were not divided.

'O my Lord Jesus,' prayed Francis, 'I beseech Thee, grant me *two* graces before I die; the *first*, that I may feel in my soul and in my body, as far as may be, the pain that Thou, sweet Lord, didst bear in the hours of Thy most bitter passion; the *second*, that I may feel in my heart, as far as may be, that exceeding love wherewith Thou, O Son of God, didst willingly endure such agony for us sinners.'

His prayer was answered. As the sun was setting on a lovely autumn evening, he passed away, sharing the anguish, yet glorying in the triumph of the Cross. The song of the birds to whom he had so often preached flooded the air with the melody he loved so well.

On another beautiful evening, nearly seven centuries later, Matthew Arnold passed suddenly away. It was a Sunday, and he was spending it with his brother-in-law at Liverpool. In the morning they went to Sefton Park Church. Dr. John Watson (Ian Maclaren) preached on *The Shadow of the Cross*. He used an illustration borrowed from the records of the Riviera earthquake. In one village, he said, everything was overthrown but the huge way-side crucifix, and to it the people, feeling the very ground shuddering beneath their feet, rushed for shelter and protection. After the sermon, most of the members of the congregation remained for the Communion; but Arnold went home. As he came down to lunch, a servant heard him singing softly:

> When I survey the wondrous Cross
>   On which the Prince of Glory died,
> My richest gain I count but loss,
>   And pour contempt on all my pride.
>
> Forbid it, Lord, that I should boast,
>   Save in the death of Christ my God!
> All the vain things that charm me most,
>   I sacrifice them to His blood.

In the afternoon he went for a walk with his relatives. He had, he told them, seldom been so deeply impressed by a sermon as by Dr. Watson's. He particularly mentioned the story of the Riviera crucifix. 'Yes,' he said, earnestly, 'the Cross remains, and, in the straits of the soul, makes its ancient appeal.' An hour later his heart had ceased to beat.

'*God forbid that I should glory save in the Cross!*' cried Francis.

'*The Cross remains, and, in the straits of the soul, makes its ancient appeal!*' exclaims Matthew Arnold.

For the Cross, as Francis discovered that great day, is the true source of all abiding happiness; the Cross is the stairway that Jacob saw, leading up from earth to heaven; the Cross has a charm for men of every clime and every time; it is the boast of the redeemed; the rock of ages; the hope of this world and the glory of the world to come.

XXII
EVERYBODY'S TEXT

I

Centuries seemed like seconds that day: they dwindled down to nothing. It was a beautiful September morning: I was only a little boy: and, as a great treat, my father and mother had taken me to London to witness the erection of Cleopatra's Needle. The happenings of that eventful day live in my memory as vividly as though they had occurred but yesterday. I seem even now to be watching the great granite column, smothered with its maze of hieroglyphics, as it slowly ascends from the horizontal to the perpendicular, like a giant waking and standing erect after his long, long sleep. All the way up in the train we had been talking about the wonderful thing I was so soon to see. My father had told me that it once stood in front of the great temple at Heliopolis; that the Pharaohs drove past it repeatedly on their way to and from the palace; and that, very possibly, Moses, as a boy of my own age, sat on the steps at its base learning the lessons that his tutor had prescribed. It seemed to bring Moses and me very near together. To think that he, too, had stood beside this self-same obelisk and had puzzled over the weird inscriptions that looked so bewildering to me! And now Heliopolis, the City of the Sun, has vanished! A single column tells the traveler where it stood! London is the world's metropolis to-day. And the monument, that stood among the splendors of the *old* world, is being re-erected amidst the glories of the *new*!

Will a time ever come, I wondered, when London will be as Heliopolis is? Will the Needle, in some future age, be erected in some new capital--in the metropolis of To-morrow? Had you stood, three thousand years ago, where St. Paul's now stands, the only sound that you would have heard coming up from the forests around would have been the baying of the wolves. Wild swine ranged undisturbed along the site of the Strand. But Egypt was in her glory, and the Needle stood in front of the temple! Where, I wonder, will it stand in three thousand years' time? Some such thought must have occurred to the authorities who are presiding over its erection. For see, in the base of the obelisk a huge cavity yawns! What is to be placed within it? What greeting shall we send from the ***Civilization-that-is*** to the ***Civilization-that-is-to-be***? It is a strange list upon which the officials have decided. It includes a set of coins, some specimens of weights and measures, some children's toys, a London directory, a bundle of newspapers, the photographs of the twelve most beautiful women of the period, a box of hairpins and other articles of feminine adornment, a razor, a parchment containing a translation of the hieroglyphics on the obelisk itself--the hieroglyphics that so puzzled Moses and me--and last, but not least, ***a text!*** Yes, a text; and a text, not in one language, but in every language known! The men who tear down the obelisk from among the crumbling ruins of London may not be able to decipher this language, or that, or the other. But surely one of these ten score of tongues will have a meaning for them! And so, in the speech of these two hundred and fifteen peoples, these words are written out: FOR GOD SO LOVED THE WORLD THAT HE GAVE HIS ONLY BEGOTTEN SON THAT WHOSOEVER BELIEVETH IN HIM SHOULD NOT PERISH BUT HAVE EVERLASTING LIFE. *That* is the greeting which the Twentieth Century sends to the Fiftieth! I do not know what those men--the men who rummage among the ruins of London--will make of the newspapers, the parchments, the photographs and the hairpins. I suspect that the children's toys will seem strangely familiar to them: a little girl's doll was found by the archaeologists among the ruins of Babylon: childhood keeps pretty much the same all through the ages. But the text! The text will seem to those far-off people as fresh as the latest fiftieth-century sensation. Those stately cadences belong to no particular time and to no particular clime. Ages may come and go; empires may rise and fall; they will still speak with fadeless charm to the hungry hearts of men. They are for the Nations-that-were, for the Nations-that-are, and for the Nations-yet-to-be. That Text is ***EVERYBODY'S TEXT***.

II

Few things are more arresting than the way in which these tremendous words have won the hearts of all kinds and conditions of men. I have been reading lately the lives of some of our most eminent evangelists and missionaries; and nothing has impressed me more than the conspicuous part that this text has played in their personal lives and public ministries. Let me reach down a few of these volumes.

Here is the *Life of Richard Weaver*. In the days immediately preceding his conversion, Richard was a drunken and dissolute coal miner. It is a rough, almost repulsive, story. He tells us how, after his revels and fights, he would go home to his mother with bruised and bleeding face. She always received him tenderly; bathed his wounds; helped him to bed; and then murmured in his ear the words that at last seemed inseparable from the sound of her voice: **God so loved the world that He gave His only begotten Son that whosoever believeth in Him should not perish but have everlasting life.** The words came back to him in the hour of his greatest need. His soul was passing through deep waters. Filled with misery and shame, and terrified lest he should have sinned beyond the possibility of salvation, he crept into a disused sand-pit. He was engaged to fight another man that day, but he was in death-grips with a more terrible adversary. 'In that old sand-pit,' he says, 'I had a battle with the devil; and I came off more than conqueror through Him that loved me.' And it was the text that did it. As he agonized there in the sand-pit, tormented by a thousand doubts, his mother's text all at once spoke out bravely. It left no room for uncertainty. '**God so loved the world that He gave His only begotten Son that whosoever believeth in Him should not perish, but have everlasting life.**' 'I thought,' Richard tells us, 'that *whosoever* meant *me*. What faith was, I could not tell; but I had heard that it was taking God at His word; and so I took God at His word and trusted in the finished work of my Saviour. The happiness I then enjoyed I cannot describe; my peace flowed as a river.'

Duncan Matheson and Richard Weaver were contemporaries. They were born at about the same time; and, at about the same time they were converted. Matheson was Scottish; Weaver was English. Matheson was a stonemason; Weaver was a coal-miner; in due course both became evangelists. In some respects they were as unlike each other as two men could possibly be: in other respects their lives are like sister ships; they seem exactly alike. Especially do they resemble each other in their earliest religious experiences. We have heard Weaver's story: let us turn to Matheson's. Weaver, at the time of his conversion, was twenty-five: Matheson is twenty-two. He has been ill at ease for some time, and every sermon he has heard has only deepened his distress. On a sharp winter's morning, with the frost sparkling on the shrubs and plants around him, he is standing in his father's garden, when, suddenly, the words of Richard Weaver's text--Everybody's Text--take powerful hold upon his mind. 'I saw,' he says, 'that God loves me, for God loves all the world. I saw the proof of His love in the giving of His Son. I saw that *whosoever* meant *me*, *even me*. My load was loosed from off my back. Bunyan describes his pilgrim as giving three leaps for joy as his burden rolled into the open sepulchre. I could not contain myself for gladness.' The parallel is very striking.

'***God loves me!*** *exclaims* Richard Weaver, in surprise.

'*I saw that God loves me!*' says Duncan Matheson.

'*I thought that "whosoever" meant "me"*' says Weaver.

'*I saw that "whosoever" meant "me,"*' says Matheson.

'*The happiness I then enjoyed I cannot describe*,' says our English coal-miner.

'*I could not contain myself for gladness*,' says our Scottish stonemason.

We may dismiss the evangelists with that, and turn to the missionaries.

III

Like Richard Weaver and Duncan Matheson, Frederick Arnot and Egerton R. Young were contemporaries. I heard them both--Fred Arnot in Exeter Hall and Egerton Young in New Zealand. They lived and labored on opposite sides of the Atlantic. Fred Arnot gave himself to the fierce Barotses of Central Africa; Egerton Young set himself to win the Red Men of the North American woods and prairies.

Arnot's life is one of the most pathetic romances that even Africa has given to the world. He made the wildest men love him. Sir Francis de Winton declares that

Arnot made the name of Englishman fragrant amidst the vilest habitations of cruelty. 'He lived a life of great hardship,' says Sir Ralph Williams; 'I have seen many missionaries under varied circumstances, but such an absolutely forlorn man, existing on from day to day, almost homeless, without any of the appliances that make life bearable, I have never seen.' And the secret of this great unselfish life? The secret was the text. He was only six when he heard Livingstone. He at once vowed that he, too, would go to Africa. When his friends asked how he would get there, he replied that, if that were all, he would swim. But nobody knew better than he did that the real obstacles that stood between himself and a life like Livingstone's were not physical but spiritual. He could not lead Africa into the kingdom of Christ unless he had first entered that kingdom himself. As a boy of ten, he found himself lying awake at two o'clock one morning, repeating a text. He went over it again and again and again. ***God so loved the world that He gave His only begotten Son that whosoever believeth in Him should not perish but have everlasting life.*** 'This,' says Sir William Robertson Nicoll, 'was Arnot's lifelong creed, and he worked in its spirit.' 'This,' he says himself, 'was my first and chief message.' He could imagine none greater.

Exactly so was it with Egerton Young. He tells us, for example, of the way in which he invaded the Nelson River district and opened work among people who had never before heard the gospel. He is surrounded by two hundred and fifty or three hundred wild Indians. 'I read aloud,' he says, 'those sublime words: ***For God so loved the world that He gave His only begotten Son that whosoever believeth in Him should not perish but have everlasting life.*** They listened with the most rapt attention whilst for four hours I talked to them of the truths of this glorious verse. When I had finished, every eye turned towards the principal chief. He rose, and, coming near me, delivered one of the most thrilling addresses I have ever heard. Years have passed away since that hour, and yet the memory of that tall, straight, impassioned Indian is as vivid as ever. His actions were many, but all were graceful. His voice was particularly fine and full of pathos, for he spoke from the heart.'

'"Missionary," exclaimed the stately old chief, "I have not, for a long time, believed in our religion. I hear God in the thunder, in the tempest and in the storm: I see His power in the lightning that shivers the tree: I see His goodness in giving us the moose, the reindeer, the beaver, and the bear. I see His loving-kindness in sending us, when the south winds blow, the ducks and geese; and when the snow and ice melt away, and our lakes and rivers are open again, I see how He fills them with fish. I have watched all this for years, and I have felt that the Great Spirit, so kind and watchful and loving, could not be pleased by the beating of the conjurer's drum or the shaking of the rattle of the medicine man. And so I have had no religion. But what you have just said fills my heart and satisfies its longings. I am so glad you have come with this wonderful story. Stay as long as you can!'"

Other chiefs followed in similar strains; and each such statement was welcomed by the assembled Indians with vigorous applause. The message of the text was the very word that they had all been waiting for.

Fred Arnot found that it was what **Africa** was waiting for!

Egerton Young found that it was what **America** was waiting for!

It is the word that **all the world** is waiting for!

For that text is *Everybody's Text*!

IV

A pair of evangelists--Weaver and Matheson!

A pair of missionaries--Arnot and Young!

I have one other pair of witnesses waiting to testify that this text is *Everybody's Text*. Martin Luther and Lord Cairns have very little in common. One was German; the other was English. One was born in the fifteenth century; the other in the nineteenth. One was a monk; the other was Lord Chancellor. But they had *this* in common, that they had to die. And when they came to die, they turned their faces in the same direction. Lord Cairns, with his parting breath, quietly but clearly repeated the words of *Everybody's Text*. ***God so loved the world that He gave His only begotten Son that whosoever believeth in Him should not perish but have everlasting life.***

During his last illness, Luther was troubled with severe headaches. Someone recommended to him an expensive medicine. Luther smiled.

'No,' he said, 'my best prescription for head and heart is that ***God so loved*** *the world that He gave His only begotten Son that whosoever believeth in Him should not perish but have everlasting life.*'

A fortnight before he passed away, he repeated the text with evident ecstasy, and added, 'What Spartan saying can be compared with this wonderful brevity? It is a Bible in itself!' And in his dying moments he again repeated the words, thrice over, in Latin.

'They are the best prescription for headache and heartache!' said Luther.

There were headaches and heartaches in the world three thousand years ago, when Cleopatra's Needle stood beside the Temple at Heliopolis!

There will be headaches and heartaches in the world centuries hence, when the obelisk is rescued from among the ruins of London!

There were headaches and heartaches among those Barotse tribes to whom Fred Arnot went!

There were headaches and heartaches among those tattooed braves to whom Egerton Young carried the message!

There are headaches and heartaches in England, as the Lord Chancellor knew!

There are headaches and heartaches in Germany, as Luther found!

And, because there are headaches and heartaches for everybody, this is **Everybody's Text**. There is, as Luther said, nothing like it.

V

When Sir Harry Lauder was here in Melbourne, he had just sustained the loss of his only son. His boy had fallen at the front. And, with this in mind, Sir Harry told a beautiful and touching story. 'A man came to my dressing-room in a New York theater,' he said, 'and told of an experience that had recently befallen him. In American towns, any household that had given a son to the war was entitled to place a star on the window-pane. Well, a few nights before he came to see me, this man was walking down a certain avenue in New York accompanied by his wee boy. The lad became very interested in the lighted windows of the houses, and clapped his hands when he saw the star. As they passed house after house, he would say, "Oh, look, Daddy, there's another house that has given a son to the war! And there's another! There's one with two stars! And look! there's a house with no star at all!" At last they came to a break in the houses. Through the gap could be seen the evening star shining brightly in the sky. The little fellow caught his breath. "Oh, look, Daddy," he cried, "God must have given *His* Son, for He has got a star in *His* window."'

'He has, indeed!' said Sir Harry Lauder, in repeating the story.

But it took the clear eyes of a little child to discover that the very stars are repeating *Everybody's Text*. The heavens themselves are telling of the love that gave a Saviour to die for the sins of the world.

www.bookjungle.com *email: sales@bookjungle.com fax: 630-214-0564 mail: Book Jungle PO Box 2226 Champaign, IL 61825*

The Codes Of Hammurabi And Moses
W. W. Davies

QTY

The discovery of the Hammurabi Code is one of the greatest achievements of archaeology, and is of paramount interest, not only to the student of the Bible, but also to all those interested in ancient history...

Religion   **ISBN:** *1-59462-338-4*   Pages:132
MSRP *$12.95*

The Theory of Moral Sentiments
Adam Smith

QTY

This work from 1749. contains original theories of conscience amd moral judgment and it is the foundation for systemof morals.

Philosophy   **ISBN:** *1-59462-777-0*   Pages:536
MSRP *$19.95*

Jessica's First Prayer
Hesba Stretton

QTY

In a screened and secluded corner of one of the many railway-bridges which span the streets of London there could be seen a few years ago, from five o'clock every morning until half past eight, a tidily set-out coffee-stall, consisting of a trestle and board, upon which stood two large tin cans, with a small fire of charcoal burning under each so as to keep the coffee boiling during the early hours of the morning when the work-people were thronging into the city on their way to their daily toil…

Childrens   **ISBN:** *1-59462-373-2*   Pages:84
MSRP *$9.95*

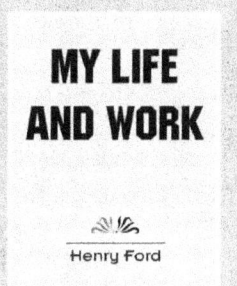

My Life and Work
Henry Ford

QTY

Henry Ford revolutionized the world with his implementation of mass production for the Model T automobile. Gain valuable business insight into his life and work with his own auto-biography… "We have only started on our development of our country we have not as yet, with all our talk of wonderful progress, done more than scratch the surface. The progress has been wonderful enough but…"

Biographies/   **ISBN:** *1-59462-198-5*   Pages:300
MSRP *$21.95*

www.bookjungle.com email: sales@bookjungle.com fax: 630-214-0564 mail: Book Jungle PO Box 2226 Champaign, IL 61825

The Art of Cross-Examination
Francis Wellman

QTY

I presume it is the experience of every author, after his first book is published upon an important subject, to be almost overwhelmed with a wealth of ideas and illustrations which could readily have been included in his book, and which to his own mind, at least, seem to make a second edition inevitable. Such certainly was the case with me; and when the first edition had reached its sixth impression in five months, I rejoiced to learn that it seemed to my publishers that the book had met with a sufficiently favorable reception to justify a second and considerably enlarged edition. ..

Reference   ISBN: *1-59462-647-2*   **Pages:412** **MSRP $19.95**

On the Duty of Civil Disobedience
Henry David Thoreau

QTY

Thoreau wrote his famous essay, On the Duty of Civil Disobedience, as a protest against an unjust but popular war and the immoral but popular institution of slave-owning. He did more than write—he declined to pay his taxes, and was hauled off to gaol in consequence. Who can say how much this refusal of his hastened the end of the war and of slavery ?

Law   ISBN: *1-59462-747-9*   **Pages:48** **MSRP $7.45**

Dream Psychology Psychoanalysis for Beginners
Sigmund Freud

QTY

Sigmund Freud, born Sigismund Schlomo Freud (May 6, 1856 - September 23, 1939), was a Jewish-Austrian neurologist and psychiatrist who co-founded the psychoanalytic school of psychology. Freud is best known for his theories of the unconscious mind, especially involving the mechanism of repression; his redefinition of sexual desire as mobile and directed towards a wide variety of objects; and his therapeutic techniques, especially his understanding of transference in the therapeutic relationship and the presumed value of dreams as sources of insight into unconscious desires.

Psychology   ISBN: *1-59462-905-6*   **Pages:196** **MSRP $15.45**

The Miracle of Right Thought
Orison Swett Marden

QTY

Believe with all of your heart that you will do what you were made to do. When the mind has once formed the habit of holding cheerful, happy, prosperous pictures, it will not be easy to form the opposite habit. It does not matter how improbable or how far away this realization may see, or how dark the prospects may be, if we visualize them as best we can, as vividly as possible, hold tenaciously to them and vigorously struggle to attain them, they will gradually become actualized, realized in the life. But a desire, a longing without endeavor, a yearning abandoned or held indifferently will vanish without realization.

Self Help   ISBN: *1-59462-644-8*   **Pages:360** **MSRP $25.45**

www.bookjungle.com *email: sales@bookjungle.com fax: 630-214-0564 mail: Book Jungle PO Box 2226 Champaign, IL 61825*

QTY

- [ ] **The Rosicrucian Cosmo-Conception Mystic Christianity** by **Max Heindel** ISBN: *1-59462-188-8* **$38.95**
  The Rosicrucian Cosmo-conception is not dogmatic, neither does it appeal to any other authority than the reason of the student. It is: not controversial, but is: sent forth in the, hope that it may help to clear... New Age/Religion Pages 646

- [ ] **Abandonment To Divine Providence** by **Jean-Pierre de Caussade** ISBN: *1-59462-228-0* **$25.95**
  "The Rev. Jean Pierre de Caussade was one of the most remarkable spiritual writers of the Society of Jesus in France in the 18th Century. His death took place at Toulouse in 1751. His works have gone through many editions and have been republished... Inspirational/Religion Pages 400

- [ ] **Mental Chemistry** by **Charles Haanel** ISBN: *1-59462-192-6* **$23.95**
  Mental Chemistry allows the change of material conditions by combining and appropriately utilizing the power of the mind. Much like applied chemistry creates something new and unique out of careful combinations of chemicals the mastery of mental chemistry... New Age Pages 354

- [ ] **The Letters of Robert Browning and Elizabeth Barret Barrett 1845-1846 vol II** ISBN: *1-59462-193-4* **$35.95**
  by **Robert Browning** and **Elizabeth Barrett** Biographies Pages 596

- [ ] **Gleanings In Genesis (volume I)** by **Arthur W. Pink** ISBN: *1-59462-130-6* **$27.45**
  Appropriately has Genesis been termed "the seed plot of the Bible" for in it we have, in germ form, almost all of the great doctrines which are afterwards fully developed in the books of Scripture which follow... Religion/Inspirational Pages 420

- [ ] **The Master Key** by **L. W. de Laurence** ISBN: *1-59462-001-6* **$30.95**
  In no branch of human knowledge has there been a more lively increase of the spirit of research during the past few years than in the study of Psychology, Concentration and Mental Discipline. The requests for authentic lessons in Thought Control, Mental Discipline and... New Age/Business Pages 422

- [ ] **The Lesser Key Of Solomon Goetia** by **L. W. de Laurence** ISBN: *1-59462-092-X* **$9.95**
  This translation of the first book of the "Lemegton" which is now for the first time made accessible to students of Talismanic Magic was done, after careful collation and edition, from numerous Ancient Manuscripts in Hebrew, Latin, and French... New Age/Occult Pages 92

- [ ] **Rubaiyat Of Omar Khayyam** by **Edward Fitzgerald** ISBN: *1-59462-332-5* **$13.95**
  Edward Fitzgerald, whom the world has already learned, in spite of his own efforts to remain within the shadow of anonymity, to look upon as one of the rarest poets of the century, was born at Bredfield, in Suffolk, on the 31st of March, 1809. He was the third son of John Purcell... Music Pages 172

- [ ] **Ancient Law** by **Henry Maine** ISBN: *1-59462-128-4* **$29.95**
  The chief object of the following pages is to indicate some of the earliest ideas of mankind, as they are reflected in Ancient Law, and to point out the relation of those ideas to modern thought. Religion/History Pages 452

- [ ] **Far-Away Stories** by **William J. Locke** ISBN: *1-59462-129-2* **$19.45**
  "Good wine needs no bush, but a collection of mixed vintages does. And this book is just such a collection. Some of the stories I do not want to remain buried for ever in the museum files of dead magazine-numbers an author's not unpardonable vanity..." Fiction Pages 272

- [ ] **Life of David Crockett** by **David Crockett** ISBN: *1-59462-250-7* **$27.45**
  "Colonel David Crockett was one of the most remarkable men of the times in which he lived. Born in humble life, but gifted with a strong will, an indomitable courage, and unremitting perseverance... Biographies/New Age Pages 424

- [ ] **Lip-Reading** by **Edward Nitchie** ISBN: *1-59462-206-X* **$25.95**
  Edward B. Nitchie, founder of the New York School for the Hard of Hearing, now the Nitchie School of Lip-Reading, Inc, wrote "LIP-READING Principles and Practice". The development and perfecting of this meritorious work on lip-reading was an undertaking... How-to Pages 400

- [ ] **A Handbook of Suggestive Therapeutics, Applied Hypnotism, Psychic Science** ISBN: *1-59462-214-0* **$24.95**
  by **Henry Munro** Health/New Age/Health/Self-help Pages 376

- [ ] **A Doll's House: and Two Other Plays** by **Henrik Ibsen** ISBN: *1-59462-112-8* **$19.95**
  Henrik Ibsen created this classic when in revolutionary 1848 Rome. Introducing some striking concepts in playwriting for the realist genre, this play has been studied the world over. Fiction/Classics/Plays 308

- [ ] **The Light of Asia** by **sir Edwin Arnold** ISBN: *1-59462-204-3* **$13.95**
  In this poetic masterpiece, Edwin Arnold describes the life and teachings of Buddha. The man who was to become known as Buddha to the world was born as Prince Gautama of India but he rejected the worldly riches and abandoned the reigns of power when... Religion/History/Biographies Pages 170

- [ ] **The Complete Works of Guy de Maupassant** by **Guy de Maupassant** ISBN: *1-59462-157-8* **$16.95**
  "For days and days, nights and nights, I had dreamed of that first kiss which was to consecrate our engagement, and I knew not on what spot I should put my lips..." Fiction/Classics Pages 240

- [ ] **The Art of Cross-Examination** by **Francis L. Wellman** ISBN: *1-59462-309-0* **$26.95**
  Written by a renowned trial lawyer, Wellman imparts his experience and uses case studies to explain how to use psychology to extract desired information through questioning. How-to/Science/Reference Pages 408

- [ ] **Answered or Unanswered?** by **Louisa Vaughan** ISBN: *1-59462-248-5* **$10.95**
  Miracles of Faith in China Religion Pages 112

- [ ] **The Edinburgh Lectures on Mental Science (1909)** by **Thomas** ISBN: *1-59462-008-3* **$11.95**
  This book contains the substance of a course of lectures recently given by the writer in the Queen Street Hall, Edinburgh. Its purpose is to indicate the Natural Principles governing the relation between Mental Action and Material Conditions... New Age/Psychology Pages 148

- [ ] **Ayesha** by **H. Rider Haggard** ISBN: *1-59462-301-5* **$24.95**
  Verily and indeed it is the unexpected that happens! Probably if there was one person upon the earth from whom the Editor of this, and of a certain previous history, did not expect to hear again... Classics Pages 380

- [ ] **Ayala's Angel** by **Anthony Trollope** ISBN: *1-59462-352-X* **$29.95**
  The two girls were both pretty, but Lucy who was twenty-one who supposed to be simple and comparatively unattractive, whereas Ayala was credited, as her Bombwhat romantic name might show, with poetic charm and a taste for romance. Ayala when her father died was nineteen... Fiction Pages 484

- [ ] **The American Commonwealth** by **James Bryce** ISBN: *1-59462-286-8* **$34.45**
  An interpretation of American democratic political theory. It examines political mechanics and society from the perspective of Scotsman James Bryce Politics Pages 572

- [ ] **Stories of the Pilgrims** by **Margaret P. Pumphrey** ISBN: *1-59462-116-0* **$17.95**
  This book explores pilgrims religious oppression in England as well as their escape to Holland and eventual crossing to America on the Mayflower, and their early days in New England... History Pages 268

www.bookjungle.com *email: sales@bookjungle.com fax: 630-214-0564 mail: Book Jungle PO Box 2226 Champaign, IL 61825*

QTY

The Fasting Cure *by Sinclair Upton* **ISBN:** *1-59462-222-1* **$13.95**
In the Cosmopolitan Magazine for May, 1910, and in the Contemporary Review (London) for April, 1910, I published an article dealing with my experiences in fasting. I have written a great many magazine articles, but never one which attracted so much attention... *New Age/Self Help/Health Pages 164*

Hebrew Astrology *by Sepharial* **ISBN:** *1-59462-308-2* **$13.45**
In these days of advanced thinking it is a matter of common observation that we have left many of the old landmarks behind and that we are now pressing forward to greater heights and to a wider horizon than that which represented the mind-content of our progenitors... *Astrology Pages 144*

Thought Vibration or The Law of Attraction in the Thought World **ISBN:** *1-59462-127-6* **$12.95**
by William Walker Atkinson *Psychology/Religion Pages 144*

Optimism *by Helen Keller* **ISBN:** *1-59462-108-X* **$15.95**
Helen Keller was blind, deaf, and mute since 19 months old, yet famously learned how to overcome these handicaps, communicate with the world, and spread her lectures promoting optimism. An inspiring read for everyone... *Biographies/Inspirational Pages 84*

Sara Crewe *by Frances Burnett* **ISBN:** *1-59462-360-0* **$9.45**
In the first place, Miss Minchin lived in London. Her home was a large, dull, tall one, in a large, dull square, where all the houses were alike, and all the sparrows were alike, and where all the door-knockers made the same heavy sound... *Childrens/Classic Pages 88*

The Autobiography of Benjamin Franklin *by Benjamin Franklin* **ISBN:** *1-59462-135-7* **$24.95**
The Autobiography of Benjamin Franklin has probably been more extensively read than any other American historical work, and no other book of its kind has had such ups and downs of fortune. Franklin lived for many years in England, where he was agent... *Biographies/History Pages 332*

Name

Email

Telephone

Address

City, State ZIP

☐ **Credit Card** ☐ **Check / Money Order**

Credit Card Number

Expiration Date

Signature

Please Mail to: Book Jungle
PO Box 2226
Champaign, IL 61825
or Fax to: 630-214-0564

ORDERING INFORMATION

web: *www.bookjungle.com*
email: *sales@bookjungle.com*
fax: *630-214-0564*
mail: *Book Jungle PO Box 2226 Champaign, IL 61825*
or PayPal *to sales@bookjungle.com*

Please contact us for bulk discounts

DIRECT-ORDER TERMS

**20% Discount if You Order
Two or More Books**
Free Domestic Shipping!
Accepted: Master Card, Visa,
Discover, American Express

www.ingramcontent.com/pod-product-compliance
Lightning Source LLC
Chambersburg PA
CBHW081837170426
43199CB00017B/2762